Paving Your Path™
What's Next For High School Graduates **COMPANION WORKBOOK**
A Promotion Protocol Guide To Manifesting Career Success
Copyright © 2019 by Kim Nugent, Ed.D.
This book can be purchased in bulk at a wholesale discount via IngramSpark. It is also available internationally via Amazon.com.

ALL RIGHTS RESERVED. This book contains material protected under International and Federal Copyright Laws and Treaties. Any unauthorized reprint or use of this material is prohibited. No part of this book may be reproduced or transmitted in any form or by any means, electronic or mechanical, including photocopying, recording, or by any information storage and retrieval system without express written permission from the author/publisher.

Publisher: Unfold Your Success, LLC
Paperback ISBN: 978-0-578-61543-1

Contact Kim Nugent, Ed.D at:
Email: Kim@PromotionProtocol.com
Web: PromotionProtocol.com | DrNugentSpeaks.com | DrKimNugent.com

Credits:
Cover Designs, Interior Layout & Design: Gagan Sarkaria, M.F.A., M.B.A.
https://GaganSarkaria.com | https://UnfoldYourSuccess.com
Book Cover Sales Copy & Content Editing: Gagan Sarkaria

Paving Your Path Complete Branding, Art Direction, Design, Production, and Online Business Development by The Branding Expert: Gagan Sarkaria

Author Photo: Lisa Crosby
Impression Consultant: Andy Paige

PAVING YOUR PATH

What's Next For High School Graduates

Companion Workbook

Kim Nugent, Ed.D
Mentoring A New Generation of Exceptional Leaders
A Promotion Protocol Guide To Manifesting Career Success

PAVING YOUR PATH COMPANION WORKBOOK

TABLE OF CONTENTS

MENTEE-MENTOR AGREEMENT 9

- 13   MENTEE PREPARATION
- 15   SELF-ASSESSMENT INVENTORY
- 21   PATHWAYU™
- 23   MENTORING SCHEDULE

THE SOLUTION FOR A NEW GENERATION 27

- 31   A IS FOR ATTITUDE
- 41   B IS FOR BRAND
- 55   C IS FOR COMMUNICATION
- 65   D IS FOR DEPTH
- 75   E IS FOR EMOTIONAL INTELLIGENCE
- 87   F IS FOR FOCUS
- 95   G IS FOR GRATITUDE
- 105   H IS FOR HABITS
- 117   I IS FOR INTEGRITY

129	J IS FOR JADED	
139	K IS FOR KNOWLEDGEABLE	
151	L IS FOR LIFE-LONG LEARNER	
163	M IS FOR MINDSET	
177	N IS FOR NETWORK	
189	O IS FOR OPPORTUNITY	
197	P IS FOR PROBLEM-SOLVER	
207	Q IS FOR QUESTION	
217	R IS FOR RESPONSIBILITY	
229	S IS FOR SELF-AWARENESS	
241	T IS FOR THANK YOU	
251	U IS FOR UNIQUE	
261	V IS FOR VISION	
271	W IS FOR WHITE LIES	
299	Z IS FOR ZONE	

SELF-ASSESSMENT INVENTORY: POST ASSESSMENT — **307**

313   THE FINAL MENTOR-MENTEE MEETING

ONLINE RESOURCES — **315**

REFERENCES — **317**

ABOUT THE AUTHOR — **325**

PAVING YOUR PATH: WHAT'S NEXT FOR HIGH SCHOOL GRADUATES

"The delicate balance of mentoring someone is not creating them in your own image, but giving them the opportunity to create themselves.

—Steven Spielberg

MENTEE-MENTOR AGREEMENT

We are both excited about embarking on this journey together. We both want this to be a rewarding experience, spending most of our time discussing developmental activities that will provide valuable knowledge in the future. We agree that...

1. The mentoring relationship will last for six (6-7) months. If for some reason it does not meet the needs of the mentee, we can decide to end the formal relationship at any time through a conversation.

2. We will meet once-a-week. Meeting times once agreed, should not be cancelled unless this is unavoidable. At the end of each meeting, we will agree on a date for the next meeting.

3. Each meeting can range from thirty (30) minutes to sixty (60) minutes. (The mentor and mentee should choose what is best for both parties.)

4. If the mentee has questions during the week, check in with the mentor by text/email, so you get your questions answered. The mentor can

also check in to see how the mentee is doing throughout the week.

5. The aim of the partnership is to discuss the following goals:

a)

b)

c)

6. We agree that the role of the mentor is to:

• Provide guidance, share ideas and provide feedback.

• Act as a sounding board for ideas/concerns about career choices.

• Identify resources to help enhance personal development and career growth.

• Serve as an advocate for mentee whenever the opportunity presents itself.

7. We agree that the role of the mentee is to:

• Identify the skills, knowledge and/or goals you want to achieve and communicate with your mentor.

• Maintain a mentoring plan and work with your mentor to set up goals, developmental activities, and time frames.

• Work with your mentor to see resources for learning: identify people and information that might be helpful.

8. We agree to keep the content of these meetings confidential.

9. The mentor agrees to be honest and provide constructive feedback. to the mentee. The mentee agrees to be open to the feedback.

Date:

_____

Mentor's signature:

_____

Mentee's signature:

_____

MENTEE PREPARATION
GETTING TO KNOW YOU GUIDE

The intention of the Getting to Know You Guide is for the student to answer these questions before the initial meeting with their mentor. It helps set the stage for engaging in meaningful dialogue. As the mentor, have the student fill out the Getting to Know You Guide before your next meeting. Ideally, it would be your initial meeting, or it could take several sessions. You both decide what is best.

Getting to Know You Guide to Provide to the Mentor

Name: _____

High School: _____

Grade Level: _____

Email address: _____

Cell Phone: _____

SELF-ASSESSMENT INVENTORY
INSTRUCTIONS

What if we created a win-win situation? Let's begin by starting the self-assessment inventory. Please take it before you embark on this mentoring journey; let's determine how self-aware you are at this point.

If you are the student and are reading this to determine what is next after high school, please begin by completing the self-assessment. In the appropriate area, rate yourself in each category from 1 to 10, 1 being poor and 10 being excellent. Do not skip any of the twenty-six categories. Save the second column for your weekly mentoring meetings.

If you are the mentor, schedule weekly coaching meetings. These meetings can be face-to-face, by telephone or Skype. Read through the questions before you meet with the student, so you have a sense of where you want to take the conversation. Feel free to enhance the questions based on your experience.

This approach will help you mentor a new generation of aspiring leaders. Know that by using this approach you are leaving a legacy for our high school students to manifest their destiny.

SELF-ASSESSMENT INVENTORY

ABC's of Possibilities	Plan to improve/Resources utilized
Rate Yourself 1–10. 1 being poor and 10 being excellent.	
1 2 3 4 5 6 7 8 9 10 Attitude: What is your attitude?	
1 2 3 4 5 6 7 8 9 10 Brand: How are you known? What impression do you make face-to-face or through social media?	
1 2 3 4 5 6 7 8 9 10 Communication: How effective are your communications skills?	
1 2 3 4 5 6 7 8 9 10 Depth: What is your personal depth? What do you know?	
1 2 3 4 5 6 7 8 9 10 Emotional Intelligence: What is your emotional intelligence quotient?	

PAVING YOUR PATH: WHAT'S NEXT FOR HIGH SCHOOL GRADUATES

ABC's of Possibilities	Plan to improve/Resources utilized
Rate Yourself 1–10. 1 being poor and 10 being excellent.	
1 2 3 4 5 6 7 8 9 10 Focused: How focused are you?	
1 2 3 4 5 6 7 8 9 10 Gratitude: How grateful are you?	
1 2 3 4 5 6 7 8 9 10 Habits: How effective are your habits?	
1 2 3 4 5 6 7 8 9 10 Integrity: How well do you keep your word to yourself and others?	
1 2 3 4 5 6 7 8 9 10 Jaded: Are there areas in your life where you feel jaded?	
1 2 3 4 5 6 7 8 9 10 Knowledgeable: How knowledgeable are you?	

ABC's of Possibilities	Plan to improve/Resources utilized
Rate Yourself 1–10. 1 being poor and 10 being excellent.	
1 2 3 4 5 6 7 8 9 10 Life-Long Learning: How committed are you to life-long learning?	
1 2 3 4 5 6 7 8 9 10 Mindset: Do you have a growth- or fixed-mindset?	
1 2 3 4 5 6 7 8 9 10 Network: How strong is your social network?	
1 2 3 4 5 6 7 8 9 10 Opportunity: Do you see life as an opportunity?	
1 2 3 4 5 6 7 8 9 10 Problem-Solver: How effective are your problem-solving skills? Do you tend to be logical and have a process or are you emotional?	

PAVING YOUR PATH: WHAT'S NEXT FOR HIGH SCHOOL GRADUATES

ABC's of Possibilities	Plan to improve/Resources utilized
Rate Yourself 1–10. 1 being poor and 10 being excellent.	
1 2 3 4 5 6 7 8 9 10 Question: How effective are your questioning skills?	
1 2 3 4 5 6 7 8 9 10 Responsibility: How strong is your sense of responsibility?	
1 2 3 4 5 6 7 8 9 10 Self-Awareness: How self-aware are you?	
1 2 3 4 5 6 7 8 9 10 Thank You: How appreciative are you? Do you always say thank you?	
1 2 3 4 5 6 7 8 9 10 Unique: How unique are you?	
1 2 3 4 5 6 7 8 9 10 Vision: Have you created a vision for your life?	

ABC's of Possibilities	Plan to improve/Resources utilized
1 2 3 4 5 6 7 8 9 10 White-Lies: Do you find yourself telling white-lies and justifying them?	
1 2 3 4 5 6 7 8 9 10 X-Factor: What is the X-factor you bring?	
1 2 3 4 5 6 7 8 9 10 Yearning: Do you have a real yearning for life?	
1 2 3 4 5 6 7 8 9 10 Zone: Do you feel you are in the zone?	

PATHWAYU™
STUDENT SUCCESS FROM ENROLLMENT TO RETIREMENT ASSESSMENT TOOL

PathwayU™ is an evidence-based assessment tool to discern your calling and live your purpose. The process takes about 20 – 25 minutes. Take your time to reflect as you answer the questions. You will complete 4 assessments. They are interests, values, personality and workplace preferences. You will receive personalized assessment reports. You will enjoy exploring the career matches to see what education and career matches are a great fit or you.

You will reflect on your purpose and your intention on what you want to accomplish which is something that matters deeply to you and benefits the world. Your calling can be described as a pathway for expressing your purpose in ways that can make the world better.

Start your journey by accessing the link through:

https://PromotionProtocol.PathwayU.com

There is a nominal fee for this assessment, which has been heavily discounted. Access is granted ongoingly.

In addition, there are robust career development tools included such as tips for resumes, interviewing and networking. There is also a job board that can be accessed through your interests and zip code in the United States. This is incredibly helpful if you plan on moving throughout your life. Prepare for your future by learning about your gifts and the type of environment you need to succeed.

> "When something is important enough, you do it even if the odds are not in your favor.
> —Elon Musk, South African-American technology entrepreneur, investor, engineer, Founder and CEO of SpaceX, Co-Founder and CEO of Tesla, Inc.

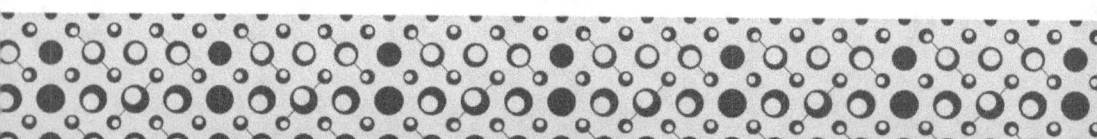

MENTORING SCHEDULE

Week 1:

    (a) Initial Intake Meeting. Mentee asks Mentor to take on this role.
    (b) Mentor completes Mentoring agreement form, checklist.
    (c) Mentee completes the Getting to Know you Guide and emails to mentor.
    (d) Mentor and mentee review the agreement form and sign.

Week 2: Mentor and mentee

    (a) Overview of the first six chapters.
    (b) Mentee completes the self-awareness inventory and gives to the mentor as a baseline.
    (c) Consider taking the education/career assessment located at https://promotionprotocol.pathwayu.com

Weeks 3 to 14:

    (a) A – M Sections. Read one article a week starting with A.

(b) Complete the mentee questions and mentor questions.
(c) Take notes.
(d) Acknowledge the progress to date. Thank each other.

Week 15:

(a) Mid-point review and map out deliverables for the pathway selected (University, community college, career-focused school, military, full-time employment, entrepreneurship).

Weeks 16-29:

(a) N – Z Sections. Read one article a week starting with N.
(b) Complete the mentee questions and mentor questions.
(c) Take notes.

Week 30:

(a) Final meeting. Review of all deliverables.
(b) Celebrate.

There are enormous benefits of mentoring for both the mentee and the mentor. For the mentee, it can result in a better attitude about school, help you uncover your blind spots, improve your interpersonal skills, develop stronger relationships and provide you with a greater sense of confidence and self-esteem. For the mentor, the benefits can include a sense of accomplishment and contribution, a greater insight into adolescence and young adulthood, and increased patience.

PAVING YOUR PATH: WHAT'S NEXT FOR HIGH SCHOOL GRADUATES

THE SOLUTION FOR A NEW GENERATION
ABC'S OF POSSIBILITIES

If certain leadership traits can be agreed upon, we can have a common ground for shared expectations. As the mentor, how can you enhance your mentoring skills? As the student, how can you reap the benefits of having a mentor? What if we created a Win-Win? Let's start now. It is time to take the self-assessment and begin our journey together.

Ideally, you will take the Self-Awareness Inventory in your junior year of high school but is never too late to get started. So, let's make your journey real! Let's examine where you are right now. I have created a guide to work on specific traits to enhance your potential regardless of the pathway you choose. I call them the **ABC's of Possibilities.**

Let's get started. Review the list of tips. How well did you do? What areas could be improved? Create a self-improvement plan. Start NOW! That future could come sooner than you think.

The framework of this book is to set up weekly mentoring meetings. The student should read and answer all the self-assessment questions

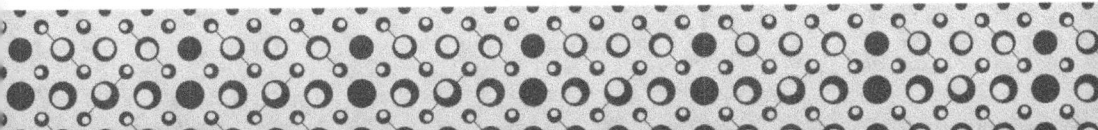

starting in week three with the letter A, which is for Attitude.

This is the prep work for the mentoring session. The mentor will come to the meeting having reviewed the week's questions. Many of the questions each week will be similar. Both sets are questions written out for transparency purposes, so there are no surprises for either party. The mentor always has the flexibility to add or modify the questions based on experience, relationship, and context.

> " Life belongs to the living, and he who lives must be prepared for changes.
> —Johann Wolfgang von Goethe, German Poet

PAVING YOUR PATH: WHAT'S NEXT FOR HIGH SCHOOL GRADUATES

ATTITUDE

> "Ability is what you are capable of doing; Motivation determines what you can do; Attitude determines how well you do it.
> —Lou Holtz, Former football player, coach and analyst

A IS FOR ATTITUDE

On any given day, school can be challenging for anyone. Our attitude reflects who we are. How important do you think having a positive and professional attitude is? What is your mood each day when you arrive at school or when you get home? What about throughout the day? Do people like to be around you? Do you bring a positive outlook or do people avoid you? Do you bring others down? Are you hanging around friends with negative attitudes that bring you down? Do you find yourself complaining about homework or teachers? Do people make excuses for you, such as saying, "Well that is just the way he is" or try and avoid him? Are you an energy drain on the team? Don't be a Debbie Downer or a Ned Know It All.

Jon Gordon wrote an article called, *How to Deal with Energy Vampires* after writing his book *The Energy Bus.* The point is you do not want to be known at school or at home as an energy vampire. A person who sucks the air out of the room. You feel bored, overwhelmed, and frustrated by them. These people exist. Make sure you are not one of them. Remember, bad attitudes are contagious, and so are good ones. How would people you are friends with describe your attitude?

According to the dictionary, the definition of attitude is a way of thinking or feeling expressed through behaviors. Attitude can be expressed in a variety of ways such as job satisfaction, productivity, innovation, respect, helpfulness, and overall morale within the department.

Attitude is fundamental to your success. It is a social "soft skill." There are many excellent assessments online that you could take to form a baseline if you do not feel you are as self-aware as you would like to be. Assessments can include attitude, emotional intelligence, leadership skills, etc.

We all have blind spots, so the more you begin to uncover yours and take action steps to improve, the more confident you will be, and more possibilities will arise. Start out each day with a gratitude journal or positive meditation or affirmations. Write out the things you are grateful for such as your family, friends, health, etc. Be specific. The more consistent you are with starting each day like this, the more your attitude will improve. Taking small steps each day creates an improved attitude. Once you find the beauty in the little things, your universe seems to expand in higher proportion.

Examine the language you use. Is it positive or negative? If it tends to be negative, start by rephrasing. Think before you say anything out loud. If you are feeling angry or frustrated breathe before you speak. Surround yourself with positive people. Don't you love being around positive people? Look for the good in people. I know positive people inspire and motivate me. They make me smile. Do you make others smile?

Do good work without expecting anything in return. Be willing to forgive. Learn from your mistakes and do not beat yourself up mentally.

When you make a mistake, get in the habit of thinking through what you learned and then move on. Do not dwell on negative things, people, or conversations. I believe part of my professional success is I do not dwell on problems. I get into action and work towards a solution. My advice is to get into action, and a change in attitude will follow.

John C. Maxwell wrote a book, titled *Attitude 101: What Every Leader Needs to Know*. This book is a practical guide and a great place to start examining your thoughts, feelings, and behaviors at work. You can determine your circumstances by maintaining a positive attitude. You can take your first step toward leadership by improving your attitude at work, with family, and friends. It starts with you!

RESOURCES:

Attitude 101: What Every Leader Needs to Know by John Maxwell.

The Energy Bus by Jon Gordon.

How to Deal with an Energy Vampire by Jon Gordon http://www.jongordon.com/positive-tip-energy-vampires.html

The Attitude Test: https://www.3smartcubes.com/pages/tests/attitudetest/attitudetest_instructions/Online attitude assessments

Why Attitude is Everything by Les Brown and Jim Rohn https://www.youtube.com/watch?v=nbfFDnKkMvw

KIM NUGENT, ED.D.

Self-Assessment Questions

Date: _____   **Week:** _____

Learning goals:

Q: How self-aware are you?
Response:

Q: Have you ever taken an attitude assessment?
Response:

Q: Have you ever had a 360-degree performance assessment in your life? If yes, what did it reveal?
Response:

Q: If you were to ask your friends about your attitude, what would they say? Interview 3 to 5 people you trust that will give you direct feedback about your attitude. Ask for tips to improve.
Response:

PAVING YOUR PATH: WHAT'S NEXT FOR HIGH SCHOOL GRADUATES

Q: What would your teachers say regarding your attitude? If you do not know, ask.

Response:

Q: What would your family say about your attitude? If you do not know, ask.

Response:

Q: When you hit a roadblock at work, how do you handle it?

Response:

Q: Do you feel like you are resilient? If yes, give an example.

Response:

Q: If you get off track or get stressed out, how do you get yourself back on track?
Response:

Q: In what area do you think you excel?
Response:

Q: Based on the feedback you received, what is one area in which you could improve your attitude?
Response:

Q: What is one action step you can take to improve in this area?
Response:

PAVING YOUR PATH: WHAT'S NEXT FOR HIGH SCHOOL GRADUATES

Q: How will you know you are making progress?
Response:

Q: Journal any extra thoughts, questions, or concerns.
Response:

KIM NUGENT, ED.D.

Mentor Questions

Date: _____   **Week:** _____

This session objectives:

Q: Describe your attitude from the self-assessment inventory.
Response:

Q: Did you ask others for feedback about your attitude? How many people and who were they?
Response:

Q: Did you learn anything new?
Response:

Q: What is one action step you can take to improve your attitude?
Response:

PAVING YOUR PATH: WHAT'S NEXT FOR HIGH SCHOOL GRADUATES

Q: How will you measure your improvement in this area?
Response:

Q: How can I support you?
Response:

Summary of key observations from today's session:

Q: What went well during the mentoring session?

Q: Were there any challenges during the session?

Q: Next action steps:

BRAND

> "Your brand is what people say about you when you are not in the room.
> —Jeff Bezos, Amazon.

B IS FOR BRAND

A brand is so much more than dressing for success. It is everything you do, every minute of the day; think of a brand as your portfolio. What does your brand say about you? What does your brand say to people in your life each day? What impression do you think you are making? Are you consistent? It is the way you dress, your image, how you communicate, your etiquette, and the way you carry yourself. Your brand is a walking billboard of everything you do, communicate, project, how you serve others and what you wear.

A brand is a way of personally marketing yourself in your career. So, before you can build your brand in person and through social media, you have to be self-aware. As you grow and develop, you can build your brand. Think of it like this you are either building your brand or tearing it down.

In the area of social media, think about where you post and what you post. What would your family, teachers or employers say about these posts? Would they believe you demonstrate a quality brand? Or would they think they would never write a recommendation letter for you or even hire you? Conduct your own social media audit. List all accounts and go back and review your posts. Is there anything you have posted in the past that you regret? Are your profiles complete? Your posts on social media are your digital fingerprint, and it follows you throughout your life.

The reality is, your posts can help or harm you. Some prospective employees were not offered positions because of Facebook and other social media postings. Examples of such posts are Saturday night party shots, foul language, provocative dress, etc. Whether you like it or not, nothing is off the record. Big brother really is watching.

On the other hand, some prospective employees were hired because of their strong brands, posts, and contributions they made on their social media accounts. Examples of posts include a professional photo of yourself, volunteer work such as the Food Bank, Habitat for Humanity, family outings, etc. These demonstrate strong values.

LinkedIn is a most effective business tool. Take the time to build your profile. Learn how to do this. There are books, online resources, other LinkedIn profiles, and LinkedIn University to help you. Do you have a professional photograph for your social media accounts? Is your résumé updated? How strong are your connections? How did you invite them? How many groups do you belong to? What videos, articles, or pictures are you posting/sharing? Do you have a strong headline? Do you blog or post, so you can be seen as a thought leader? Do you have strong recommendations for you on your LinkedIn profile? These recommendations on LinkedIn can enhance your visibility. Choose wisely when asking for professional recommendations. Start thinking now about having at least three professional recommendations. Ask.

Then stay in touch with these people.

Many years ago, I worked for an organization as President in one of the operating units. The President of the parent corporation was leaving, and I knew him well. He knew my work well. I asked him for a recommendation on LinkedIn when I was first setting up my profile. Honestly, I never thought about it again. Fast forward six years; I had left my company and was interviewing for a new position with a new company. I was flown to Chicago for a face-to-face interview. While I was waiting, the Human Resources recruiter came and talked with me. The first thing she said was, "I checked out your LinkedIn profile." She added, "You have impressive recommendations." I had forgotten entirely about those recommendations. The man who was going to interview me for a new position with a new company was the former President of the parent corporation I had worked for those many years ago. It is obvious these recommendations helped me get an opportunity to interview. Oh, and yes, I did get the new job!

Beyond social media is your brand at work. How do you show up? Are you helpful? Do you consistently do your best work? Do you dress professionally every day? Do you read your emails before you hit "send" to make sure there are no typos? Do you send professional messages? No one can be an expert in everything, so ask questions. Seek out more experienced people and learn from them. Seek out thought leaders and observe what they do. You are unique, so capitalize on your strengths.

There are so many great places to seek out how to improve your brand. In 1997, Fast Company Magazine featured the article *"The Brand Called You"* written by Tom Peters. To deepen your understanding, check out this article to learn how you can improve your brand. Your brand is your reputation every day.

RESOURCES:

The Brand Called You by Tom Peters https://www.fastcompany.com/28905/brand-called-you

Personal Image Presence: Professional Image Audit (Online profile) https://www.evansville.edu/careercenter/downloads/ProfessionalImageSelfAudit.pdf?v=2

Social Media Audit Template https://blog.hootsuite.com/social-media-audit-template/

PAVING YOUR PATH: WHAT'S NEXT FOR HIGH SCHOOL GRADUATES

Self-Assessment Questions

Date: _____   **Week:** _____

Learning goals:

Q: What does your brand communicate about you?
Response:

Q: What would people say about you, if you were not in the room? If you do not know, ask 3 to 5 people.
Response:

Q: How self-aware are you about your brand? 1 being poor and 10 being excellent.
Response:

Q: On a scale of 1-10, how strong is your brand?
Response:
1. Face-to-face, what impression are you making?
2. Communication
3. Social Media accounts

PAVING YOUR PATH: WHAT'S NEXT FOR HIGH SCHOOL GRADUATES

Q: What is one area in which you could improve your brand?

Response:

Q: Have you set up a LinkedIn profile? How can it be improved?

Response:

Q: What is one area in which you could improve your brand on your social media accounts? Is there anything you have posted in the past that might have you concerned?

Response:

Q: How will you learn more about developing your personal brand?

Response:

Q: What is one action step you can take to improve your brand?
Response:

Q: How will you know you are making progress?
Response:

Q: Journal any extra thoughts, questions, or concerns.
Response:

"Image and perception are the only two things that create value. Without an image there is no perception.
–Gagan Sarkaria, High Achievement Book, Branding and Business Coach

Mentor Questions

Date: _____   **Week:** _____

This session objectives:

Q: Describe your brand's self-assessment.
Response:

Q: What did you learn from the Fast Company article on *The Brand Called You* by Tom Peters?
Response:

Q: Did you ask others for constructive feedback about the impression you make?
Response:

Q: Did you ask others for feedback on your social media accounts?
Response:

PAVING YOUR PATH: WHAT'S NEXT FOR HIGH SCHOOL GRADUATES

Q: Did you learn anything new?
Response:

Q: Did any comments surprise you?
Response:

Q: Have you set up a LinkedIn profile? If yes, may I review your LinkedIn profile, I think I can offer some suggestions. Are you open to this type of feedback?
Response:

Q: What is one action you can take to improve in this area?
Response:

Q: How will you measure your improvement in this area?
Response:

Q: How can I support you?
Response:

Summary of key observations from today's session:

Q: What went well during the mentoring session?

Q: Were there any challenges during the session?

Q: Next action steps:

" There is always space for improvement, no matter how long you've been in the business.
—Oscar De La Hoya, American athlete

COMMUNICATION

> "I think for any relationship to be successful, there must be loving communication, appreciation, and understanding.
> —Miranda Kerr, Australian model

C IS FOR COMMUNICATION

How effective are your communication skills? People judge others within seconds, often based on speaking skills. Do you relate well to others – peers, staff members, teachers, and parents? Do you struggle with how to get your meaning across to others? Do you get nervous? Do you overshare details of your personal life?

Depending on your communication level, check out the following organizations to enhance your confidence and communication skills: Dale Carnegie Training, Toastmasters International, and National Speakers Association (NSA) in your area. Located in major cities, Dale Carnegie is an excellent organization that specializes in public-speaking training. Toastmasters International is a great organization to join in your local area to practice your speaking skills. National Speakers Association is for professional speakers and those who often speak in their leadership positions, which is something you can strive for later in your career. You can watch YouTube videos that model excellent communication skills. There are also apps to help you improve your communication skills such as VoiceThread and Paper Telephone.

What about your writing skills? Are your emails, texts, and presentations clear and appropriate for the intended receiver or audience? Have you ever created confusion by your poorly worded emails and texts? Do you read, use spell-check and resources such as Grammarly© before hitting the "send" button? If writing is a weakness, it can be improved with deliberate practice. We can all improve our communication skills no matter who we are. There are many significant online resources to help you develop, so check them out. You do not want to create a negative impression from behind your computer, without ever leaving your office.

What about your listening skills? Do you wait for the person to finish what they are saying before you talk or interrupt? Listen to understand. Are you thinking about what you are going to say without paying attention to what the other person is saying? Have you learned to ask questions instead of always talking? Ask open-ended questions. This is a skill that must be practiced. If you do not think so, let me ask you a question. Have you ever played the telephone game? It is a game of five people. You tell the first person something, and they must repeat it to the next person. By the time you get to the fifth person, the original conversation is not at all the same conversation. This is how rumors start, just because of poor listening skills and rephrasing. As your listening improves, so will all your relationships. There are personal-development classes that are offered to help you progress in this area.

While all these skills are critical to career success, most communication models suggest that 7% is verbal communication and 93% of our communication is non-verbal. The 93% is broken down into 55% body language and 38% tone of voice (Mehrabian, 1972, p. 1).

Poor communication skills create problems for you. As you have reviewed A, B and C which are A-Attitude, B-Brand, and C-Communication, how would you assess yourself? Where are your opportunities for self-improvement? You have taken the first three steps to become more aware of who you are and who you can become.

Let's keep going!

RESOURCES:

Communication Model by Albert Mehrabian https://www.toolshero.com/communication-skills/communication-model-mehrabian/

Communication Skills: How to Improve Communication Skills 7 Tips https://www.youtube.com/watch?v=mPRUNGGORDo

Dale Carnegie https://www.dalecarnegie.com/en/topics/people-skills

Improve your Listening Skills with Active Listening by Mindtools.com https://www.youtube.com/watch?v=t2z9mdX1j4A

National Speakers Association https://www.nsaspeaker.org/attend/chapter-directory/

Toastmasters https://www.toastmasters.org/

KIM NUGENT, ED.D.

Self-Assessment Questions

Date: _____ **Week:** _____

Learning goals:

Q: Rate your communication skills on a scale of 1–10 with 1 being poor and 10 being excellent.

Response:

_____Listening   _____Asking questions

_____Speaking   _____Nonverbal Communication

_____Writing   _____Body Language

_____Presenting   _____Tone of Voice

Q: What is an area you need to start on first?

Response:

Q: In what area could you improve your communication skills at school? In what area could your communication skills improve at work?

Response:

Q: What outside resources will help you improve in this area?

Response:

Q: Have you ever participated in Toastmasters, Dale Carnegie, watched YouTube videos on the subject, used communication apps or personal-development courses to improve your communication?
Response:

Q: How will you know you are making progress?
Response:

Q: Journal any extra thoughts, questions, or concerns.
Response:

KIM NUGENT, ED.D.

Mentor Questions

Date: _____   **Week:** _____

This session objectives:

Q: Describe your communication skill strengths.
Response:

Q: Describe your communication skill weaknesses.
Response:

Q: How important do you think effective communication skills are for life?
Response:

Q: Have you ever participated in Toastmasters, Dale Carnegie, watched YouTube videos on the subject, used communication apps or personal development courses to improve your communication?
Response:

•••
Q: Are you open to participating in one of the above activities to improve?
Response:

•••
Q: What is one action you can take to improve in this area?
Response:

Q: How will you measure your improvement in this area?
Response:

Q: How can I support you?
Response:

Summary of key observations from today's session:

Q: What went well during the mentoring session?

Q: Were there any challenges during the session?

Q: Next action steps:

"Take advantage of every opportunity to practice your communication skills so that when important occasions arise, you will have the gift, the style, the sharpness, the clarity, and the emotions to affect other people.

—Jim Rohn, American entrepreneur, author and motivational speaker

DEPTH

> "Well, I believe that the depth of your struggle can determine the height of your success. I was inspired to come out of everything I've been through and end up in a place I never thought I would be.
> —Robert Sylvester Kelly, American singer, song writer, record & former professional basketball player

D IS FOR DEPTH

Do you have depth? To get the most out of life, it is essential to have depth and breadth. Are you driven for a more significant purpose in life? Have you traveled to other parts of the world and applied what you learned to your life? Do you interact with all different types of people? Do you try and experience new things? Do you take a variety of classes? Do you read, listen to podcasts, and seek more knowledge? Do you speak more than one language? Are you working part-time or hold an internship position? Do you do volunteer work? Do you participate in extra-curricular activities or are you a student leader of an organization?

Do you seek to build your character? Have you developed your creativity such as writing, painting, dancing, or playing an instrument? If not, what is the obstacle? What do you tell yourself? With whom do you surround yourself; positive people who encourage you and challenge you; or people who will bring you down and add no value?

According to Mark Myhre (2005), writer and emotional healing coach, depth is defined as a way to add richness and beauty to our lives. While you might not have ever read "depth" as being a trait in a leadership book, it is a critical trait. So how can you develop more depth? Depth can be acquired over a lifetime every day, by challenging the status quo regarding learning new things, expanding your character, and seeking purpose and meaning to life. You are looking to expand your thinking and your interests. You have a variety of interests and become more interesting as you share with others. As you do this, your energy expands, and you become more self-actualized.

Depth takes consistent action. It is not "do one thing and stop." It is not getting a degree in philosophy. It is getting in touch with what you value. It is expanding your knowledge in all areas of your life and sharing it. It is fun exploring and challenging your attitude, knowledge, and skills. Depth allows you to experience new things without judgment or expectation. Depth gives you the opportunity to connect with people at a deeper level. It is not being shallow.

Be open to new opportunities. Be open to meeting new people. Be open to travel. Think about saying yes more often than you say no. Think about the reasons you give yourself when you say no. What might happen if you answered "yes" the next time? You might be surprised how much you have in common with others if you take the time to get to know them. Show people what you value in them.

RESOURCES:

Myhre, Mark (2005). *Developing Personal Depth.* http://www.articlecity.com/articles/self_improvement_and_motivation/article_3237.shtml

PAVING YOUR PATH: WHAT'S NEXT FOR HIGH SCHOOL GRADUATES

What resources can you bring to this strategy? For example: Books, articles, online resources, or programs.

_____
_____
_____
_____
_____
_____
_____

Self-Assessment Questions

Date: _____   **Week:** _____

Learning goals:

Q: In what areas do you need to expand your personal depth?
Response:

Q: What is an area of interest that you want to explore or deepen first?
Response:

Q: What is one area where you could improve your creativity or right brain?
Response:

Q: What is one area you could improve your business or career knowledge, or left brain at work?
Response:

PAVING YOUR PATH: WHAT'S NEXT FOR HIGH SCHOOL GRADUATES

Q: How will you know you are making progress?
Response:

Q: Journal any extra thoughts, questions, or concerns.
Response:

Mentor Questions

Date: _____   **Week:** _____

This session objectives:

• •

Q: Describe how you have developed your personal depth and interests at this point in yourself.

Response:

• •

Q: What area are you excited about expanding?

Response:

• •

Q: What area are you nervous about expanding?

Response:

• •

Q: What area in your life have you noticed you say "no" to instead of "yes"?

Response:

Q: Where have you said "no" in your life that you might be open to answering "yes" now?
Response:

Q: Tell me more about the reason you have not tried it or what you tell yourself you cannot do?
Response:

Q: What is one action you can take to improve in this area?
Response:

Q: How will you measure your improvement in this area?
Response:

Q: How can I support you?
Response:

Summary of key observations from today's session:

Q: What went well during the mentoring session?

Q: Were there any challenges during the session?

Q: Next action steps:

> "Once we accept our limits, we go beyond them.
> — Albert Einstein, German physicist

EMOTIONAL INTELLIGENCE

" When our emotional health is in a sad state, so is our level of self-esteem. We have to slow down and deal with what is troubling us so that we can enjoy the pure joy of being happy and at peace with ourselves.
—Jess C. Scott, Author artist and non-conformist

E IS FOR EMOTIONAL INTELLIGENCE

We all experience emotions. What we do with those emotions differentiates us from others. You might know that IQ (Intelligence Quotient) is important, but EQ (Emotional Intelligence; Emotional Quotient) is even more critical. Mike Robbins, (2018) author, *Bring Your Whole Self to Work*, shared that Jeff the talent manager at Adobe as part of his introduction as a keynote speaker, said, "Your IQ might get you in the door, but EQ is what will get you promoted." Daniel Goleman noted that a leader's success is two thirds emotional intelligence and one-third IQ. So, what does that mean to you in your life?

When our emotions are not under control, we take actions we might not usually make. Emotions are comprised of feelings that result in physical and psychological changes that influence thought and behavior. What is emotional intelligence? It is the ability to be intelligent with our emotions. It is the capacity to be able to be aware of, control and express one's emotions and to handle relationships with others well. Emotional intelligence is made up of a combination of personal competence and social competence. Under personal competence it is self-awareness and self-management. Under social competence, it is social awareness and relationship management.

• Self-awareness is the ability to recognize and understand your own emotions as they happen and appreciate your general tendencies for responding to and defending people and situations.

• Social awareness is understanding where the other person is coming from whether you agree or not.

• Self-management is using awareness of your emotions to choose what you say and do to positively direct your behavior and manage your reactions.

• Relationship management is using awareness of the other person's emotions to choose what you say and do to positively direct your behavior.

Emotional intelligence takes time to develop. It is a skill that needs to be developed and practiced. As a teen, your brain is still developing, and your emotions and impulses may not be understood entirely by you right now. Think about a person who you admire that model's emotional intelligence. See what you can learn from them. Also, to become more self-aware, take a free online emotional intelligence assessment or read Daniel Goleman's book on Emotional Intelligence.

What are the benefits to you in becoming more emotionally intelligent? You can improve your relationships, feel more confident, become more self-aware, be less impulsive, possess the ability to be happier more often and have developed social skills (Nalin, 2017, P. 4).

RESOURCES:

Emotional Intelligence Test by The Global Leadership Foundation https://globalleadershipfoundation.com/geit/eitest.html

Emotional Intelligence YouTube video by The Life School https://www.youtube.com/watch?v=LgUCyWhJf6s

Emotional Intelligence YouTube video with Daniel Goleman https://www.youtube.com/watch?v=Y7m9eNoB3NU

KIM NUGENT, ED.D.

Self-Assessment Questions

Date: _____   **Week:** _____

Learning goals:

Q: Take the EI online assessment. What did you learn about yourself after you took the EI assessment?
Response:

Q: How do you feel today? What is the reason you feel this way?
Response:

Q: Describe how you see yourself. Include your strengths, weaknesses, emotions, and motivation. Do you have an overall positive or negative impression of yourself?
Response:

PAVING YOUR PATH: WHAT'S NEXT FOR HIGH SCHOOL GRADUATES

Q: Write out your first name and last name. Using the letters of your name, create words that express your positive traits.

Response:

Q: Write about a time when you let your emotions take over? How did your reactions make you feel afterward?

Response:

Q: What triggers stress for you? Do you know when it is coming on? Do you know how to manage it?

Response:

Q: What are your expectations for school and work relationships?
Response:

Q: How will you know you are making progress?
Response:

Q: Journal any extra thoughts, questions, or concerns.
Response:

"You can either see yourself as a wave in the ocean or you can see yourself as the ocean.

—Oprah Winfrey, American entertainer

Mentor Questions

Date: _____   **Week:** _____

This session objectives:

....

Q: What did you learn about yourself after you took the EI assessment?
Response:

....

Q: Complete the following:
Response:

I am most happy when

I feel embarrassed when

I think negative thoughts about myself when

....

Q: How do you think emotional intelligence will impact your life?
Response:

....

Q: Describe how you see yourself. Include your strengths, weaknesses, emotions, and motivation. Do you have an overall positive or negative impression of yourself?
Response:

Q: Tell me about a time when you let your emotions take over? How did your reactions make you feel afterward?

Response:

Q: What causes you to lose your cool? How do you manage your anger?

Response:

Q: What triggers stress for you? Do you know when it is coming on? Do you know how to manage it?

Response:

Q: How long does it take for you to get frustrated or angry?

Response:

Q: What are your expectations for school and work relationships?
Response:

Q: What is one action you can take to improve in this area?
Response:

Q: How will you measure your improvement in this area?
Response:

Q: How can I support you?
Response:

Summary of key observations from today's session:

Q: What went well during the mentoring session?

Q: Were there any challenges during the session?

Q: Next action steps:

"Empathy and social skills are social intelligence, the interpersonal part of emotional intelligence. That's why they look alike.
—Daniel Goleman, American psychologist, science journalist and author of the best-selling book Emotional Intelligence.

FOCUS

> "You can do anything as long as you have the passion, the drive, the focus, and the support.
> —Sabrina Bryan, Singer, actress, author, dancer, fashion designer, choreographer

F IS FOR FOCUS

Do you find it difficult to focus in this fast-paced world with competing priorities, deadlines, phones, social media, etc.? Do you ever wish you could ignore the distractions? It is imperative that you focus on being successful at school, at home, and in life. Easier said than done.

Also, many students today have ADHD and find it extra tough to stay focused, but some strategies can help. If this is you, your teacher or doctor may have specific strategies to help. In some cases, some students have found online high school programs can eliminate distractions and boost academic achievement.

The truth is, our attention spans are becoming shorter and shorter, but it is possible to work on improving your focus. While we all have been told that multitasking is excellent, the reality is that you can only do one thing at a time well. There are reasons we all have trouble focusing. It could be physical (low energy, dehydration), phone, computer, siblings, parents, internal thoughts, a difficult task, low motivation or low sense of urgency (Wray, 2018, p. 2.).

First, make a list of things that distract you and keep them to a minimum or eliminate them. Have a planner or electronic calendar. Block out time on your calendar for projects. Schedule the deadline date on the calendar and work backward to make sure you fulfill your part of the project on time. Do not schedule every minute of the day. Take short breaks every so often to re-energize.

Know when your energy level is at its highest for you. Is it morning, afternoon or evening? Schedule homework when your energy level is high. Make sure you have water close by to stay hydrated and try exercising 15 minutes before you study to give your system a boost. You might need to stand or walk to stay focused instead of sitting. Take short breaks. Studying for long periods of time is not productive.

Do not log into your social media accounts while at school or when doing homework. They distract and eat up valuable time. Turn off your phone when doing homework. Find a quiet place to study if possible. If silence is distracting, play music that helps you focus. Don't check email regularly. Get in the habit now of checking only three times a day. Answer the emails, delete, or file for follow up. Deal with emails one at a time. Where do you find yourself wasting time throughout the day? Can you make better use of your lunch period or free period to do homework, so you do not have so much to do when you get home?

If you can't focus because of racing thoughts in your mind, write them down before getting started. Keeping a notepad close by will help. It will help train your brain those thoughts have been captured on paper, and you will get back to them. If you have a big project due for school, chunk it into manageable 15-minute segments. Just get started. The more you procrastinate, the more stress you have. Reward yourself when you finish your work. It might be a TV show, a movie, a video game, etc. The reward should be motivating to you.

Wasting time creates more stress and anxiety because you know you are running out of time. If procrastinating or wasting time has become a habit, analyze the reason. Do you enjoy the adrenaline rush? Some people seem to live their lives this way without stopping to see if they can change the way they manage their lives.

So, when you begin the day, have a plan. Take stock of what you want to accomplish. List out what are time wasters. Reflect on whether you need to focus more on your school, work or personal life. Breathe and get started.

RESOURCES:

Wray, M. (2014). *Creating Positive Futures: 6 simple strategies for improving student focus.* Retrieved from http://creatingpositivefutures.com/6-simple-strategies-for-improving-students-focus/

Self-Assessment Questions

Date: _____   **Week:** _____

Learning goals:

Q: Is being focused a strength or a challenge for you?
Response:

Q: In what areas do you get distracted?
Response:

Q: Do you think you are an adrenaline junkie and like the rush of waiting until the last minute?
Response:

Q: How can you reduce these distractions from happening? Reduce your addiction to stress?
Response:

Q: What strategy can you can put in place today to help you focus?
Response:

Q: How will you know you are making progress?
Response:

Q: Journal any extra thoughts, questions, or concerns.
Response:

KIM NUGENT, ED.D.

Mentor Questions

Date: _____ **Week:** _____

This session objectives:

Q: How do you stay focused for the day?
Response:

Q: What are areas of distraction for you?
Response:

Q: What strategy can you use to help you focus going forward?
Response:

Q: How can you reduce distractions?
Response:

PAVING YOUR PATH: WHAT'S NEXT FOR HIGH SCHOOL GRADUATES

Q: What is one action you can take to improve in this area?
Response:

Q: How will you measure your improvement in this area?
Response:

Q: How can I support you?
Response:

Summary of key observations from today's session:

Q: What went well during the mentoring session?

Q: Were there any challenges during the session?

Q: Next action steps:

GRATITUDE

"Gratitude turns what we have into enough, and more. It turns denial into acceptance, chaos into order, confusion into clarity...it makes sense of our past, brings peace for today, and creates a vision for tomorrow.

—Melody Beattie, International best-selling author

G IS FOR GRATITUDE

"Gratitude" is defined as being thankful. How many times each day do we miss the opportunity to be grateful? Did you know that by practicing gratitude, your life has more meaning? It changes your perspective.

Set aside time each day and start out each day by being grateful for at least three things in your life. Either say them aloud or write them down. Keeping a gratitude journal by your bed is very helpful to start and continue this practice. Putting pen to paper is a powerful tool, as it activates your brain and senses.

So many times, we fail to acknowledge the small things we are blessed to have. Many people tend to focus on what is wrong. If you take the opposite approach and look for things for which to be grateful, you will find more and more blessings. As you write or state the things for which you are grateful, bring in all your senses. How does it make you feel? What do you see? What do you hear? What about a sense of touch?

So, what does expressing gratitude have to do with success? Everything. When you are in the workforce, there are a series of problems to solve and that causes stress. According to Robert Emmons (2004), a world's leading gratitude expert and psychology professor at the University of California Davis, "Gratitude can be that stress buster." It allows you to generate optimism while building strength to recover more quickly from setbacks. Let people in your life know you are grateful for them. Appreciate your friends and co-workers for their contribution.

According to Lindsay Holmes (2017), deputy editor for the Huffington Post, "more gratitude equals a better life." That means a better experience at home and work. If you build this habit over 30 days, you will feel grateful. Your whole outlook on life will be improved. Pass it on!

RESOURCES:

What resources can you bring to this strategy? For example: Books, articles, online resources, or programs.

_____

_____

_____

_____

_____

_____

_____

PAVING YOUR PATH: WHAT'S NEXT FOR HIGH SCHOOL GRADUATES

KIM NUGENT, ED.D.

Self-Assessment Questions

Date: _____   **Week:** _____

Learning goals:

Q: Do you keep a gratitude journal?
Response:

Q: Would you be willing to write out what you are grateful for each morning?
Response:

Q: How do you think it might change your perspective?
Response:

Q: In what areas of your life have you taken people or situations for granted?
Response:

PAVING YOUR PATH: WHAT'S NEXT FOR HIGH SCHOOL GRADUATES

Q: What can you do daily/often to express your gratitude?
Response:

Q: How will you know you are making progress?
Response:

Q: Journal any extra thoughts, questions, or concerns.
Response:

KIM NUGENT, ED.D.

Mentor Questions

Date: _____ **Week:** _____

This session objectives:

Q: What are you grateful for at school?
Response:

Q: What are you grateful for at home?
Response:

Q: What are you grateful for from your friends?
Response:

Q: What are you grateful for in your relationships?
Response:

Q: What daily practice are you willing to take to keep gratitude at the forefront?

Response:

Q: Is there any area of your life or a person you have taken for granted? Are you willing to change this? If yes, how?

Response:

Q: What is one action you can take to improve in this area?

Response:

Q: How will you measure your improvement in this area?
Response:

Q: How can I support you?
Response:

Summary of key observations from today's session:

Q: What went well during the mentoring session?

Q: Were there any challenges during the session?

Q: Next action steps:

"Relationships survive on trust, and if that is broken at any point, it's pretty much the end of the relationship. Besides, inability to communicate leads to problems.
—Yuvraj Singh, Indian athlete

HABITS

" Ninety-nine percent of the failures come from people who have the habit of making excuses.
—George Washington Carver, American scientist

H IS FOR HABITS

Do you possess good habits or bad habits? What would your friends, family, or co-workers say about your habits? You might want to interview a few trusted friends and colleagues to get an honest assessment. Often, we are blind to what we do and how it affects others.

Once again, Fast Company published an article in 2017 on bad habits to ditch. Do you possess any of these habits? *Ditch These Seven Bad Habits* before 2018 Starts by Gwen Moran. Read this article at https://www.fastcompany.com/40503547/ditch-these-seven-bad-habits-before-2018-starts and see if you see yourself as having possessed these habits.

Once we begin to recognize our bad habits, how can we start to change them? We all have them. You cannot change everything overnight, but you can take steps to improve one thing at a time. Describe your bad habit. What do you think is the root cause for it? By not doing something, what is it costing you? Or what is the payoff to you by not doing it? If you were to change it, how would it benefit your life? With what will you replace the bad habit? What can you do instead?

Once you have identified the habit, the root cause, and with what you can replace the bad habit, next is accountability. Reach out to a co-worker or friend and have them be your accountability partner. Give yourself some time. Much has been written on this subject about how long it takes to change a habit. The time-frame ranges from 21 days to six months. It depends on the habit and the person. Commit to the time-frame. Know that you probably will make a few mistakes along the way or even backslide. We are human but do not quit. No need to justify the reasons it happened but become aware of what triggered it. Recommit yourself to making progress toward changing the habit. Tomorrow is a new day!

Realize that many habits you possess are positive. Keep them and discard what does not serve you and others. You are on the road to excellence.

RESOURCES:

Ditch These Seven Bad Habits before 2018 Starts by Gwen Moran. https://www.fastcompany.com/40503547/ditch-these-seven-bad-habits-before-2018-starts

What resources can you bring to this strategy? For example: Books, articles, online resources, or programs.

_____
_____
_____
_____
_____
_____
_____

Self-Assessment Questions

Date: _____   **Week:** _____

Learning goals:

Q: What habits need to change?
Response:

Q: What new habit will you work on first?
Response:

Q: What is the underlying cause of poor habits?
Response:

Q: What is the payoff by not doing it? What is it costing you?
Response:

PAVING YOUR PATH: WHAT'S NEXT FOR HIGH SCHOOL GRADUATES

Q: Are you willing to have an accountability partner? If so, who could be your partner?

Response:

Q: What is the time-frame you are committing to change the habit?

Response:

Q: How will you celebrate your success?

Response:

Q: How will you know you are making progress?
Response:

Q: Journal any extra thoughts, questions, or concerns.
Response:

"It was character that got us out of bed, commitment that moved us into action, and discipline that enabled us to follow through.
—Zig Ziglar, American author and motivational speaker

Mentor Questions

Date: _____   Week: _____

This session objectives:

Q: What habit have you decided to work on first?
Response:

Q: How will it lead to excellence?
Response:

Q: What is the benefit of making this change?
Response:

Q: What will it cost you if you do not make the change?
Response:

PAVING YOUR PATH: WHAT'S NEXT FOR HIGH SCHOOL GRADUATES

Q: How will you feel when you change this habit?
Response:

Q: Do you have an accountability partner?
Response:

Q: How will you keep this present and at the top of your mind daily?
Response:

Q: What is your time-frame?
Response:

Q: If you make a misstep, how will you recover and get back on track?
Response:

Q: What is one action you can take to improve in this area?
Response:

Q: How will you measure your improvement in this area?
Response:

PAVING YOUR PATH: WHAT'S NEXT FOR HIGH SCHOOL GRADUATES

Q: How will we celebrate your success?
Response:

Q: How can I support you?
Response:

Summary of key observations from today's session:

Q: What went well during the mentoring session?

Q: Were there any challenges during the session?

Q: Next action steps:

INTEGRITY

> "We learned about honesty and integrity – that the truth matters...that you don't take shortcuts or play by your own set of rules…and success does not count unless you earn it fair and square.
> —Michelle Obama, American writer, lawyer and former First Lady of the U.S.

I IS FOR INTEGRITY

This is not a make-wrong word. Integrity means doing what you say you will do regardless of whether anyone is watching you or not. It is the integrity of self. Keeping and honoring your word. It is a state of being. It is keeping your promises to you, your friends, and family. You will be amazed at how free you feel when you know you can keep your word to yourself and others, and they can count on you. It does not mean always saying yes.

Here is a situation to consider: Are you great at work about keeping your word, but when it comes to yourself not so much — or vice versa? Take a real look at your life and decide where you can improve your integrity muscle. It will take practice, but each day you make an effort, you grow. Now to make this trait real, you need to dig down deep and speak truthfully to yourself.

Here are some areas to think about: Do you gossip about others? Have you taken things without paying for them? Have you taken office supplies home for personal use? Have you used the school or company copier for copying personal things? Do you tell little white lies and justify it? Do you exceed the speed limit? Have you ever parked in a handicapped accessible parking space, even though you are not handicapped? Do you think the rules do not apply to you? Have you hurt someone's feelings and never apologized? Have you been charged less for an item at a store and failed to tell them they charged you the wrong amount? Have you ever found money on the floor at a store and failed to turn it in? Have you disclosed confidential information about your family or a project? Have you used school or work time to be on social media when you were supposed to be working? Have you ever made a mistake at work and failed to own it? Did you fail to meet a company deadline? Do you follow company policies 100% of the time? Have you taken credit for someone else's work? Have you ever compromised your values? Do you have the courage, to tell the truth?

Or maybe you are great at keeping your word with others but when it comes to yourself, not as much. Do you have integrity for yourself? Do you keep your word with yourself? For example, do you tell yourself you are going to go to the gym three-days-a-week and then do not follow through? You matter.

Each day look to improve in this area. So how can you build your integrity muscle?

Be honest. When you make a mistake, own it. Be a person of your word. Become someone everyone can count on, no matter what. Know that you can rely on yourself. Know that you are your word. The more you flex the integrity muscle, the stronger you become. It is just like working out. You know you have arrived when you can count on your word and yourself. Integrity is a crucial characteristic of leadership.

Good luck getting stronger each day!

RESOURCES:

What resources can you bring to this strategy? For example: Books, articles, online resources, programs.

_____
_____
_____
_____
_____
_____
_____
_____

KIM NUGENT, ED.D.

Self-Assessment Questions

Date: _____   **Week:** _____

Learning goals:

Q: What does integrity mean to you?
Response:

Q: Is integrity important in a leadership role? Explain.
Response:

Q: When you read the examples, did you see yourself in any of them?
Response:

Q: Who do you admire because of their integrity? What company displays integrity?
Response:

Q: What examples are you aware of in business when the leader failed to have integrity? What happened? If you are not aware, research and share.
Response:

Q: What is one area that you can work on for yourself?
Response:

Q: How do you justify your behavior when your integrity is not intact?
Response:

Q: How will you know you are making progress?
Response:

Q: How will you know when you can keep your word? To yourself? To others?
Response:

Q: Journal any extra thoughts, questions, or concerns.
Response:

" Confidence... thrives on honesty, on honor, on the sacredness of obligations, on faithful protection and on unselfish performance. Without them it cannot live.
—Franklin D. Roosevelt, 32nd U.S. President

KIM NUGENT, ED.D.

Mentor Questions

Date: _____   **Week:** _____

This session objectives:

Q: What does integrity mean to you?
Response:

Q: What did you think of some of the examples provided? Let's discuss a few.
Response:

Q: Have you ever looked at integrity in this way? What surprised you?
Response:

Q: If you were in a leadership position, how would you model it?
Response:

Q: How do you demonstrate integrity currently?

Response:

Q: What happens when a leader does not model integrity? What happens to the organization? To the culture? To the people? Can you give me some specific examples?

Response:

Q: What is one action you can take to improve in this area?

Response:

Q: How will you measure your improvement in this area?
Response:

Q: How can I support you?
Response:

Summary of key observations from today's session:

Q: What went well during the mentoring session?

Q: Were there any challenges during the session?

Q: Next action steps:

PAVING YOUR PATH: WHAT'S NEXT FOR HIGH SCHOOL GRADUATES

"Honesty is the first chapter in the book of wisdom.
—Thomas Jefferson, 3rd U.S. President

JADED

"The biggest thing that people tell me is that I will be jaded real soon and that the allure of filmmaking will lose its magic. Not necessarily the fame, but that special thing you create on screen.

—Dayo Okeniyi, Nigerian American actor

J IS FOR JADED

Are you jaded because of all the negative world events? Are you feeling cynical about leadership? Do you feel disappointed by athletes and people in the media? Do you think life is not fair and you have been passed over? Do you complain about those people at work or school? Are you the person who sits in the stands and yells but does nothing or are you the person who sees a situation and wants to become an agent of change? Do you complain about your job, co-workers, boss or teachers? Or do you take the high road? Do you get involved in your community to improve the quality of life? Do you engage others to join you? Who are you in these scenarios? Are you in the stands or on the field?

According to the Merriam Webster dictionary, jaded is feeling "dull or cynical." Do you feel entitled to being cynical because you feel like you have been wronged at school or work? Do you feel like people around you are not doing their part? Did you know that being cynical is a defensive posture to try and protect yourself? But the truth is that being cynical can dramatically decrease the quality and health of your life. When you see the world from this perspective, everything is dull, and there is no joy. Probably the only person suffering is you. So, if there is an opportunity for promotion at school or your workplace, what reason would administration or leadership have for promoting someone who is cynical? I can't think of any, can you?

If you want to take the path of promotability, you might consider a different approach and begin to improve the quality of your life. You can take the high road and become an agent for change and become more positive. You can become compassionate toward others. Instead of looking for what is wrong in every situation, begin looking for what is right. Decide who you want to be. Your future is in your hands!

RESOURCES:

What resources can you bring to this strategy? For example: Books, articles, online resources, or programs.

_____

_____

_____

_____

_____

_____

_____

PAVING YOUR PATH: WHAT'S NEXT FOR HIGH SCHOOL GRADUATES

KIM NUGENT, ED.D.

Self-Assessment Questions

Date: _____   **Week:** _____

Learning goals:

Q: On a scale of 1 to 10 with 1 being feel jaded all the time, and 10 being never feel jaded. How would you rate yourself?

Response:

_____ Jaded

Q: In what areas do you struggle with cynicism?

Response:

Q: How can you begin to change this outlook?

Response:

Q: How will you know you are starting to shift your perspective?

Response:

PAVING YOUR PATH: WHAT'S NEXT FOR HIGH SCHOOL GRADUATES

Q: What is one area that you can work on for yourself?
Response:

Q: How will you know you are making progress?
Response:

Q: Journal any extra thoughts, questions, or concerns.
Response:

Mentor Questions

Date: _____ **Week:** _____

This session objectives:

Q: Are there areas at work where you feel jaded? What happened?
Response:

Q: What is the root cause?
Response:

Q: How can you change your perspective?
Response:

PAVING YOUR PATH: WHAT'S NEXT FOR HIGH SCHOOL GRADUATES

Q: If you have a friend who is jaded, how would you coach that friend? How can you propose an alternative perspective?

Response:

Q: What strategies might work to improve the situation?

Response:

Q: What resources might be available?

Response:

Q: What is one action you can take to improve in this area?

Response:

Q: How will you measure your improvement in this area?
Response:

Q: How can I support you?
Response:

Summary of key observations from today's session:

Q: What went well during the mentoring session?

Q: Were there any challenges during the session?

Q: Next action steps:

> " I think the reason I was successful is that I was never cynical.
>
> —Carol Burnett, American actress

KNOWLEDGEABLE

" Knowledge will give you power, but character respect.
—Bruce Lee, Martial artist, actor and cultural icon

K IS FOR KNOWLEDGEABLE

How prepared are you when you graduate from high school? Depending on the path you will choose, whether that is a university, community college, vocational school, military, full-time employment or entrepreneurship, you need to become more knowledgeable than you are today. Do you have a plan? What are the admissions requirements for what is next? What do you need to know? What skills or assessments do you need that you may be lacking? Are there certifications or education that would enhance your situation? How are you going to fund what is next? What do you need to research? To whom might you need to speak with?

Decide what you want to learn. Do you want to go wide or deep? Do you want to specialize in an area? Develop a plan for gaining the knowledge that you need to fill in the gaps.

Knowledge is defined as facts, information, and skills you learn through education and experience. How can you increase your knowledge? You can read. You can ask questions. You can seek out a mentor/business coach. You can follow the checklists in this book. Is there training available to enhance your skill set? Is there a student/professional organization you could join?

What can you volunteer to learn? You can stretch yourself and take on new projects to learn and assist others. Keep an open mind. It takes time to learn new things. You will make mistakes but learn from them. Notice how you feel when you are learning new things. It may be uncomfortable for a while as you are outside your comfort zone.

How can you continue to enhance your technology skills? Technology may be an area where you excel, but there is always more to learn, and it changes daily. You can also help others in this area if it is not their area of expertise. When the student becomes the teacher, you begin the path of mastery.

Examine other areas in your life where you may need to learn. Do you participate in deliberate practice and set aside time to master a new skill? What information is missing for you to increase your mastery? The only way to learn is to read, talk, practice, and then demonstrate proficiency over time.

RESOURCES:

What resources can you bring to this strategy? For example: Books, articles, online resources, or programs.

_____
_____
_____
_____
_____
_____
_____
_____

KIM NUGENT, ED.D.

Self-Assessment Questions

Date: _____   Week: _____

Learning goals:

Q: Depending on the path you choose upon graduation, on a scale of 1 to 10, with 1 being not clear and 10 being really clear, how well do you understand the entrance requirements?

Response:

_____University   _____Entrepreneurship
_____Community College   _____Finances/Budget
_____Vocational School   _____Technology
_____Military   _____Community Service/AmeriCorps
_____Full-Time Employment

Q: Once you have completed the list, decide where to start. What is the first action step to increase your knowledge?

Response:

Q: What is your plan to gain more knowledge? Write out the plan and be ready to share with your mentor. This is a crucial conversation.

Response:

PAVING YOUR PATH: WHAT'S NEXT FOR HIGH SCHOOL GRADUATES

Q: What way do you learn best? Check all that apply.
Response:

____Visual (V)   ____Blended learning
____Auditory (A)   ____Research on your own
____Read/Write (R)   ____Books
____Kinesthetic (K)   ____Podcasts
____Online   ____Workshops
____Face-to-face   ____Classes

Q: What resources are available to acquire new knowledge?
Response:

Q: How can you become ready after you graduate from high school?
Response:

Q: What is one area that you can work on for yourself?
Response:

Q: How will you know you are making progress?
Response:

Q: Journal any extra thoughts, questions, or concerns.
Response:

PAVING YOUR PATH: WHAT'S NEXT FOR HIGH SCHOOL GRADUATES

"The best preparation for tomorrow is doing your best today.

—H. Jackson Brown, Jr., American author

KIM NUGENT, ED.D.

Mentor Questions

Date: _____   **Week:** _____

This session objectives:

Q: In what areas do you feel you need to gain more knowledge about the pathway you are choosing upon graduation? Share with me your plan and list of things you need to learn so we can incorporate those into our weekly meetings.

Response:

_____University   _____Entrepreneurship
_____Community College   _____Finances/Budget
_____Vocational School   _____Technology
_____Military   _____Community Service/AmeriCorps
_____Full-Time Employment

Q: Where do you want to start? Let's create a plan.

Response:

PAVING YOUR PATH: WHAT'S NEXT FOR HIGH SCHOOL GRADUATES

Q: How do you learn best? Check all that apply.
Response:
____Visual (V)   ____Blended learning
____Auditory (A)   ____Research on your own
____Read/Write (R)   ____Books
____Kinesthetic (K)   ____Podcasts
____Online   ____Workshops
____Face-to-face   ____Classes

Q: How do you want to be coached in this area of your life?
Response:

Q: What resources do you think you need?
Response:

Q: What is one action you can take to improve in this area?
Response:

Q: How will you measure your improvement in this area?
Response:

Q: How can I support you?
Response:

Summary of key observations from today's session:

Q: What went well during the mentoring session?

Q: Were there any challenges during the session?

Q: Next action steps:

PAVING YOUR PATH: WHAT'S NEXT FOR HIGH SCHOOL GRADUATES

"Whatever you want to do, if you want to be great at it, you have to love it and be able to make sacrifices for it.

—Maya Angelou, American Poet

LIFE-LONG LEARNER

“Life is not about finding yourself. Life is about creating it.
—George Bernard Shaw, Playwright and critic

L IS FOR LIFE-LONG LEARNER

Do you love to learn? Do you have a passion for trying new things? Do you engage in learning new things both inside and outside of school? Do you look for ways to stretch your creative capacity and yourself? I often feel like a kid in the candy store when it comes to learning. I feel like there is not enough time for me to learn about all the things I am interested in, but in a good and stimulating way. I make the time because it changes me. It opens my mind to new possibilities. I use what I learn from new areas to bring back to work in my role and apply it. I learn from others and broaden my perspective. I take personal-development courses to uncover my bias or understand my thinking in more effective ways.

Learning does not even have to be formal. I take every opportunity to learn something. Here are three examples. A few years ago, I had a dental emergency, and my dentist was out of town. I went to a dentist to which my sister referred me. They took care of the problem; they were highly professional. Soon they became my dentist because of how I was treated. What impressed me most was how they made notes each time I was there. I am not talking about notes about my teeth, which would be expected. Their records were so comprehensive, and the notes included whatever we talked about whether that was family or job or travel. It was like we picked up the conversation where it left off six months prior. I think this practice is brilliant. Wouldn't it be great if every customer-service operation did the same thing?

The second example is my website provider. Their customer service is spectacular. No one is happy when they call for tech support because it means they are having a problem. The tech staff is patient; knowledgeable and has always resolved my issues 100% of the time. I share these two examples as I am looking for excellent customer-service experiences all the time, so I can bring it back to my operation and see how we can improve what we are doing. Where are you looking to learn?

The third example is my hairdresser. It is not a high-end salon, but every client is treated as a VIP. Every client is greeted when they walk through the door. They are called by name. The stylist works around the client's schedule, not the other way around. They strive to be on time. They offer refreshments. They ask questions to make sure they deliver the best result. They take nothing for granted. They set up the next appointment before the client leaves. Can you imagine how each client feels when they leave the salon? What impression do you want to make?

If you like reading, there is an excellent resource by John R. Dijulius, III (2003) a book titled: *Secret Service: Hidden Systems* that produce unforgettable customer service. These books show you a variety of companies and the systems they use to offer exceptional customer service. As I mentioned before, you can learn a lot by studying companies outside your field of study. What examples can you share related to what you have learned? What is one poor customer experience you have encountered? How did that make you feel?

Do you enjoy listening to webinars or podcasts? I love TedTalks on YouTube. You can also download the free TED app on your smart devices. If you are not familiar with TED, check it out. TED stands for Technology, Entertainment, and Design. These are 18-minute video-talks by thought leaders who present high-quality information on trending topics. Check out Ted on topics that interest you and can help you in your career. What three are your favorites?

Do you belong to student professional associations or student organizations? Are you learning a new language, or do you spend three to four hours a day on social media thinking you are learning new things to enhance your life? Expand yourself. Do something different. Make a point of learning something new every day.

RESOURCES:

Secret Service: Hidden Systems by John R. Dijulius, III (2003).

TED: Technology, Entertainment, and Design: Ideas worth spreading. https://www.ted.com

KIM NUGENT, ED.D.

Self-Assessment Questions

Date: _____　　　　　　　　　　　**Week:** _____

Learning goals:

Q: On a scale of 1 to 10 rate yourself with 1 being "I do not care to learn" and 10 being "I have a passion for learning".
Response:
_____Love of Learning

Q: What types of topics interest you?
Response:

Q: What was the last personal-development course you took?
Response:

Q: Have you watched any TedTalks? What are three of your favorites?
Response:

PAVING YOUR PATH: WHAT'S NEXT FOR HIGH SCHOOL GRADUATES

Q: What was the last book you read or listened to?
Response:

Q: What podcasts do you listen to? What type of music do you enjoy?
Response:

Q: Do you speak more than one language?
Response:

Q: What have you done to develop your creativity?
Response:

Q: What interests you?
Response:

Q: Where can lessons be learned from other industries?
Response:

Q: What customer-service examples can you provide?
Response:

Q: How can you encourage others to be life-long learners?
Response:

PAVING YOUR PATH: WHAT'S NEXT FOR HIGH SCHOOL GRADUATES

Q: What is one area that you can work on for yourself?
Response:

Q: How will you know you are making progress?
Response:

Q: Journal any extra thoughts, questions, or concerns.
Response:

Mentor Questions

Date: _____   **Week:** _____

This session objectives:

Q: How would you rate yourself on the topic of being a life-long learner? Explain.

Response:

Q: What areas of learning do you enjoy?

Response:

Q: What was the last personal development course you took?

Response:

Q: What was the last book you read or listened to?

Response:

PAVING YOUR PATH: WHAT'S NEXT FOR HIGH SCHOOL GRADUATES

Q: Do you watch TedTalks? If yes, what is one of your favorites?
Response:

Q: What podcasts do you listen to? What type of music do you enjoy?
Response:

Q: Do you speak more than one language?
Response:

Q: What have you done to develop your creativity?
Response:

Q: What topics do you find less appealing or what areas do you not like to learn about?
Response:

Q: How can you encourage others to be life-long learners?
Response:

Q: Give me two examples of excellent customer service you have received.
Response:

Give me one example of poor customer service you have received.
Response:

Q: Regarding customer service, how can we share opportunities for growth?
Response:

PAVING YOUR PATH: WHAT'S NEXT FOR HIGH SCHOOL GRADUATES

Q: What is one action you can take to improve in this area?
Response:

Q: How will you measure your improvement in this area?
Response:

Q: How can I support you?
Response:

Summary of key observations from today's session:

Q: What went well during the mentoring session?

Q: Were there any challenges during the session?

Q: Next action steps:

MINDSET

> "Innovation requires an experimental mindset.
> —Denise Morrison, Business executive

M IS FOR MINDSET

Do you have a fixed-mindset or a growth-mindset? How do you know? When you make a mistake, do you think you should stop or quit because you failed? Do you avoid risk and challenges? What do you tell yourself? When you are learning something new, and it is challenging and does not come quickly, what is your self-talk? Do you say to yourself, "It is something new to learn?" Do you want to be praised for the effort or the journey?

Mindset is defined as a set of attitudes one possesses. One of the best resources on the subject of mindset is Carol Dweck's book on *Mindset: The New Psychology of Success: How We can Fulfill our Potential*. Read it and see how you can develop a growth mindset in all areas of your life. Dr. Carol Dweck describes a fixed mindset as static, avoids challenges, sees the effort as fruitless, ignores useful negative feedback, and feels threatened by the success of others. She then describes the characteristics of a growth mindset. They are: a desire to learn, embraces challenges, is persistent, learns from criticism, and is inspired by others. Who are you?

Carol Dweck's book challenged me to examine what I was saying to my students. I realized that many of the positive things I was voicing, actually was creating a fixed mindset. I had to reframe the way I praised my students for their progress. I now praise the effort, strategies, hard work, progress, persistence and ability to learn from mistakes. I stopped saying "good job", or "you are so smart", as these are fixed ways of being. When I think about it now, my best learning came from the mistakes I made and not when I excelled.

I tested Carol Dweck's mindset theory for many years when I facilitated a graduate new-student orientation workshop each session. We had a lot of interactive activities, so the students could get the feel about what they were about to undertake in obtaining a master's degree. About midway through the orientation, I gave the graduate students an assignment. I told them at our University, every student was expected to use the American Psychological Association (APA) formatting in referencing all sources for their papers. I handed out a research paper to each student and had them try and find the APA errors. This was a tough assignment because they had not even started their classes.

I watched with intrigue how they approached the task. Most took the paper and tried to figure something out. A few took the paper and threw it to the side in total frustration. I did not let the exercise go more than two minutes for fear of them leaving before they started. I then conducted a debrief or after-action review. I asked them how they felt when I handed out the assignment. Some said they were scared, some were open to trying, and some said they felt like quitting. I told them to realize they were in graduate school to learn new things. I told them I did not really expect them to be able to do the assignment. I asked them to remember the feeling they had when we did this throughout their graduate-school journey.

I wanted to begin to create a growth mindset for every person in the workshop. If they already knew how to do these things, they would not need graduate school. It is a place to learn, to be challenged, and make mistakes. I then handed out an APA guide to help them do the assignment. We then went through the paper, and I pointed out the APA errors.

As I explained the difference and my intention, the students relaxed. They stated it was a lesson they would never forget. So how do you approach new things and what do you say to yourself?

The Biglifejournal.com created a set of questions to help you reframe your mindset. They are:

"What did you do today that made you think hard?"

"What new strategies did you try?"

"What mistake did you make that taught you something?"

"What did you try that was hard today?"

Let's take this to the world of work. What is your mindset? I often heard employees say, "These people do not like me." I have heard people say. "My boss is making me do…." I have heard, "You cannot get ahead here because…." I have never said those things as I do not see the world that way. It is not my mindset nor my self-talk. Certainly, there are workplaces where this exists, but is it really that way or is it a fixed mindset to justify your situation and make them wrong? Be mindful of your own thinking. Indeed, you are the only person who knows. As you are reading this, you may take issue with me, however, a coach challenges your thinking.

RESOURCES:

Biglifejournal.com

Mindset: The New Psychology of Success: How We can Fulfill our Potential by Carol Dweck

PAVING YOUR PATH: WHAT'S NEXT FOR HIGH SCHOOL GRADUATES

KIM NUGENT, ED.D.

Self-Assessment Questions

Date: _____   **Week:** _____

Learning goals:

Q: Overall, do you feel like you have a growth-mindset or a fixed-mindset?
Response:

Q: In what areas of your life do you have a growth-mindset?
Response:

Q: In what areas of your life do you have a fixed-mindset?
Response:

Q: Do you like to be rewarded for the outcome or the journey?
Response:

PAVING YOUR PATH: WHAT'S NEXT FOR HIGH SCHOOL GRADUATES

Q: What do you say to yourself when things are hard, or you are learning something for the very first time?

Response:

Q: How can you begin to shift your mindset to a growth-mindset?

Response:

Q: How will you know you are starting to shift your perspective?

Response:

Q: Be ready to discuss the pathway you have chosen with your mentor. Start mapping out a plan and timeframe for accomplishing them over the next 13 weeks.

Response:

Q: What is one area that you can work on for yourself?
Response:

Q: How will you know you are making progress?
Response:

Q: Journal any extra thoughts, questions, or concerns.
Response:

PAVING YOUR PATH: WHAT'S NEXT FOR HIGH SCHOOL GRADUATES

"Whatever the mind of man can conceive and believe, it can achieve.

—Napoleon Hill, American writer

Mentor Questions

Date: _____   **Week:** _____

This session objectives:

Q: Describe what you think is a growth-mindset.
Response:

Q: Describe what you think is a fixed-mindset.
Response:

Q: Do you feel like you have a growth-mindset or a fixed-mindset?
Response:

Q: In what areas of your life do you have a growth-mindset?
Response:

PAVING YOUR PATH: WHAT'S NEXT FOR HIGH SCHOOL GRADUATES

Q: In what areas of your life do you have a fixed-mindset?
Response:

Q: Do you like to be rewarded for the outcome or the journey? Explain.
Response:

Q: What do you say to yourself when things are hard, or you are learning something for the very first time?
Response:

Q: How can you begin to shift your mindset to a growth-mindset?
Response:

Q: How will you know you are starting to shift your perspective?
Response:

Q: How can I encourage your growth in this area?
Response:

Q: We are halfway through the 26 traits. What you do feel you have learned thus far?
Response:

Q: How do you feel you have changed?
Response:

Q: Now let's examine the deliverables on the pathway checklist that you have chosen and start mapping out a plan and timeframe for accomplishing them over the next 13 weeks.
Response:

PAVING YOUR PATH: WHAT'S NEXT FOR HIGH SCHOOL GRADUATES

Q: What is one action you can take to improve in this area?
Response:

Q: How will you measure your improvement in this area?
Response:

Q: How can I support you?
Response:

Summary of key observations from today's session:

Q: What went well during the mentoring session?

Q: Were there any challenges during the session?

Q: Next action steps:

NETWORK

"Virtue in obscurity is rewarded only in heaven. To succeed in this world, you have to be known to people.
—Sonia Sotomayer, American Supreme Court Justice

N IS FOR NETWORK

What is networking? Networking is where you develop business relationships, share information, and assist each other, personally and professionally. What is significant about building a network? Building a strong professional network is part of enhancing your career and business strategy. People in your network can give you advice. Determine what your purpose is and who you want to interact with. Not all events are going to be right for you. Be selective in your choices. Choose wisely when adding connections through LinkedIn, which is distinct from Facebook or other social-media choices. Stay in touch with your LinkedIn network colleagues to maintain an active network without an agenda. LinkedIn makes it very easy to stay in touch. I like to think of social media this way: LinkedIn is for business, Facebook for friends, Twitter for purpose and YouTube for subscribers.

How do I actually network? When going to a networking event, have a goal to meet one or two people. Really get to know them well. Seek out new people. Take business cards with you. I am often surprised how many people say they forgot to bring their cards. If they do not have a card, use your phone or the LinkedIn app's 'Find Nearby' feature to capture contact information. Ask them questions. Provide value; not what you want. This is not speed dating. Repeat their name. Make a note on the back of the card of when and where you met them. Follow-up within 24 hours with an email so they have a memory of you. Do not wait to do this. The goal is not to collect business cards; it is to connect. Over time you will build strong, trusting relationships. Create a win-win relationship. The more often you do this, the more confident you become.

Your network is the golden ticket to career success only if you stay in touch and build strong relationships. Look for opportunities to connect and help people in your network instead of making it all about you. Check in with them periodically to see how they are doing and see what they might need and how you might help. You will feel great when you get to help others in your network. They, one day, might be willing to help you, mentor you or endorse you.

Inc. Magazine contained an excellent article on networking called *Eight Things Power Networkers Do to Make Connections* by Minda Zetlin.

Check it out at https://www.inc.com/minda-zetlin/8-things-power-networkers-do-make-connections.html

RESOURCES:

Eight Things Power Networkers Do to Make Connections by M. Zetlin
https://www.inc.com/minda-zetlin/8-things-power-networkers-do-make-connections.html

LinkedIn. https://www.linkedin.com/feed/

PAVING YOUR PATH: WHAT'S NEXT FOR HIGH SCHOOL GRADUATES

KIM NUGENT, ED.D.

Self-Assessment Questions

Date: _____ **Week:** _____

Learning goals:

Q: What is the purpose of networking?
Response:

Q: How can it help your life or career?
Response:

Q: Do you enjoy networking?
Response:

Q: In what areas of networking do you feel you need assistance?
Response:

Q: In what areas of networking do you excel?
Response:

Q: What was the last networking or group event you attended?
Response:

Q: When and where is the next networking event you will attend?
Response:

Q: What value can you create when networking?
Response:

Q: What is one area that you can work on for yourself?
Response:

Q: How will you know you are making progress?
Response:

Q: Journal any extra thoughts, questions, or concerns.
Response:

"Effective networking isn't a result of luck – it requires hard work and persistence.
–Lewis Howes, American author

Mentor Questions

Date: _____   **Week:** _____

This session objectives:

Q: What networking events have you attended?
Response:

Q: Describe how you feel when you go to a networking or group event?
Response:

Q: Do you typically go alone to these events or do you bring another colleague, associate or friend with you?
Response:

Q: In what areas of networking do you feel you excel?
Response:

Q: In what areas of networking do you need assistance with now?
Response:

Q: Is there a networking event that you are interested in attending but have not done so yet?
Response:

Q: What is stopping you?
Response:

Q: What is one action you can take to improve in this area?
Response:

Q: How will you measure your improvement in this area?
Response:

Q: How can I support you?
Response:

Summary of key observations from today's session:

Q: What went well during the mentoring session?

Q: Were there any challenges during the session?

Q: Next action steps:

> "Learning networking basics is only a gateway to career growth and exploration.
> —Tae Yoo, American Businesswoman

OPPORTUNITY

"Success is where preparation and opportunity meet.
—Bobby Unser, American former automobile racer

O IS FOR OPPORTUNITY

Be observant. Look for opportunities to contribute and make a difference. When problems get presented, think through how you can find ways to bring value instead of complaining.

One of the best examples of this happened to me is when I first started my career in higher education as a new faculty member. I had been teaching at this school for three months before the fall session. The department director told me my class in the fall session started at 7 a.m. So, the first day of class, I arrived early, set up my class and by 7:10 a.m. no students were in class. I thought it was strange, so I headed to the Registrar's office to see the actual class schedule. The schedule said my class started at 9 a.m., not 7 a.m. I decided to just wait in the faculty/staff lounge until class was to begin. Honestly, it was the best two hours I ever spent. As each new faculty member came into the lounge, they would ask me where to turn in attendance sheets, how to use the copy machine, where were the mailboxes, the class schedule, Registrar's office, etc.? I helped each and every person even though I was new myself and did not know everything.

I went to teach my class at 9 a.m. The class ended at noon. I promptly went to the Dean of Education's office and asked to speak with him. I had only met him one time, and I was nervous. His personal assistant said he had time to see me. I explained what had occurred to me that morning, I explained a lot of new teachers were not sure what to do on the first day of class. I told him in my previous role in the hospitality industry we always held a new employee orientation before anyone started. It helped them feel better connected and more confident in the position. He said, "Great idea. You should do that." I laughed to myself, as I had not been given an orientation, but I said: "Yes, I would be happy to do this." I knew I needed to partner with someone at the school who knew the building, the programs, and all the floors. I found that person in Cliff Willson. I asked him if he would help and he said yes. So, for the next two years each quarter, we held the new-employee orientation. Each time we delivered the orientation, it became better and better.

I could have complained about the situation, but I chose a different approach. I believe that because of this situation, it propelled me into having some of the most amazing opportunities in higher education over the next 17 years.

So, think about the problems you see in your high school, college, or workplace. Reframe problems as opportunities and see where your career takes you.

RESOURCES:

What resources can you bring to this strategy? For example: Books, articles, online resources, or programs.

KIM NUGENT, ED.D.

Self-Assessment Questions

Date: _____   **Week:** _____

Learning goals:

Q: What problems or gaps have you noticed at school or job that could be viewed as opportunities?
Response:

Q: When have you taken the initiative to bring solutions to your family, school or job? Provide three examples.
Response:

Q: What kind of impact do you want to make?
Response:

PAVING YOUR PATH: WHAT'S NEXT FOR HIGH SCHOOL GRADUATES

Q: What is one area that you can work on for yourself?
Response:

Q: How will you know you are making progress?
Response:

Q: Journal any extra thoughts, questions, or concerns.
Response:

Mentor Questions

Date: _____   Week: _____

This session objectives:

Q: Did the example shared change your perspective?
Response:

Q: What problems or gaps have you noticed at school or job that could be viewed as opportunities?
Response:

Q: When have you taken the initiative to bring solutions to your family, school or job? Provide three examples.
Response:

Q: What kind of impact do you want to make?
Response:

PAVING YOUR PATH: WHAT'S NEXT FOR HIGH SCHOOL GRADUATES

Q: What is one action you can take to improve in this area?
Response:

Q: How will you measure your improvement in this area?
Response:

Q: How can I support you?
Response:

Summary of key observations from today's session:

Q: What went well during the mentoring session?

Q: Were there any challenges during the session?

Q: Next action steps:

PROBLEM-SOLVER

" Never bring the problem-solving stage into the decision-making stage. Otherwise, you surrender yourself to the problem rather than the solution.

—Robert Schuller, Pastor, motivational speaker and author

P IS FOR PROBLEM-SOLVER

Being known as a great problem solver is a life skill. People and organizations value employees, managers, and leaders who can solve problems. Since business and technology are moving at such a rapid pace, we must be able to solve problems to grow and develop; both personally and professionally.

While many of us may find ways to solve problems through trial and error, there are many other significant problem-solving models to consider. One of my favorite books on the subject was written by Thomas Connellan, Ph.D. The title of the book is *Bringing Out the Best in Others! 3 Keys for Business Leaders, Educators, Coaches, and Parents*. This is a must-read book for everyone.

My personal experience having used and taught the model is that if you use the three keys together, you really can improve performance 10 to 20%. Improvements can be made at work, on your team, and in your family. There is value in every aspect of your life by reading and applying these three keys: positive expectations, accountability/

responsibility, and feedback.

Dr. Connellan gives specific examples you can apply to your life. There are so many great and simple tips to bring about positive changes. Dr. Connellan helps to reframe the way you provide feedback to produce a better result without putting people on the defensive. He ends the book by sharing a real problem-solving model. As with any new skill, it must be practiced.

MindTools has excellent articles for career professionals. Henry Kaiser wrote one such article. Mr. Kaiser is quoted as saying, "Problems are only opportunities in work clothes." Check out the whole story at https://www.mindtools.com/pages/article/newTMC_00.htm

RESOURCES:

Bringing Out the Best in Others! 3 Keys for Business Leaders, Educators, Coaches, and Parents by T. Connellan.

What is Problem Solving? by H. Kaiser https://www.mindtools.com/pages/article/newTMC_00.htm

PAVING YOUR PATH: WHAT'S NEXT FOR HIGH SCHOOL GRADUATES

KIM NUGENT, ED.D.

Self-Assessment Questions

Date: _____   **Week:** _____

Learning goals:

Q: When problems are presented, how do you begin to solve them?
Response:

Q: Research 3 problem-solving models to help you become a better problem-solver.
Response:
a).

b).

c).

Q: What problems have you solved at work? Provide three examples.
Response:

PAVING YOUR PATH: WHAT'S NEXT FOR HIGH SCHOOL GRADUATES

Q: What is one area that you can work on for yourself?

Response:

Q: How will you know you are making progress?

Response:

Q: Journal any extra thoughts, questions, or concerns.

Response:

KIM NUGENT, ED.D.

Mentor Questions

Date: _____   Week: _____

This session objectives:

Q: When problems are presented, how do you begin to solve them?
Response:

Q: Research 3 problem-solving models to help you become a better problem-solver. Be ready to discuss the pros and cons of each approach.
Response:
a).

b).

c).

PAVING YOUR PATH: WHAT'S NEXT FOR HIGH SCHOOL GRADUATES

Q: What problems have you solved at work? Provide three examples.

Response:

Q: When you begin to solve a problem, do you look at the root cause?

Response:

Q: How do you identify the issue? How do you determine the solution(s)?

Response:

Q: How can you help your team members become better problem-solvers?

Response:

Q: What is one action you can take to improve in this area?
Response:

Q: How will you measure your improvement in this area?
Response:

Q: How can I support you?
Response:

Summary of key observations from today's session:

Q: What went well during the mentoring session?

Q: Were there any challenges during the session?

Q: Next action steps:

"Problem-solving becomes a very important part of our makeup as we grow into maturity or move up the corporate ladder.
—Zig Ziglar, American author and motivational speaker

QUESTION

> "Life is as simple as asking these questions: What do I want? Why do I want it? How will I achieve it?
> —Shannon Alder, Inspirational author

Q IS FOR QUESTION

The art of asking questions seems to be dwindling due to the fast pace of business. Taking the time to ask questions will save you time and give you the information you need to make informed decisions. Ask questions. Questions provide answers. They inform. Questions are information disguised as power. The more you ask, the more you learn about people, processes, plans, and passion. The more questions you ask, the more interesting you become. It is not in what you know, it is what you learn. If this is an area of weakness for you, learn how to ask essential questions.

There are specific types of questions for particular situations. As far back as Socrates (470-339 BC), the art of asking and answering questions was used to stimulate critical thinking. It helps inform and educate.

Organizations like the Foundation for Critical Thinking.org serve to promote asking questions and providing resources to educators, healthcare practitioners, and the military since the 1980s.

In the education industry, teachers use Blooms Taxonomy to provide questions to engage and stimulate discussions. Dr. Benjamin Bloom created the six levels of questioning in 1956. They were: knowledge, comprehension, application, analysis, synthesis, and evaluation. Anderson and Krathwohl, students of Dr. Bloom, updated Bloom's Taxonomy in 2001. The updated version is stated in terms of verbs instead of nouns to denote questioning as an action and is not static. They are: remember, understand, apply, analyze, evaluate, and create. There is also a digital version of the taxonomy to meet the needs of today's digital audience.

Even the Dale Carnegie organization believes that asking questions is an essential people skill. Check out their books and videos online. It helps inform and build connections with others. What questioning models does your organization use?

Reduce your talking, ask more questions, and increase your listening capacity. It might keep you from jumping to the wrong conclusions. If you are not listening, you are filling in the blanks with your own thoughts or meaning, which can distort the outcome of the communication.

It might surprise you how attractive you become to others when you are fully present and listening. Think about it. How do you feel when someone really listens to you?

RESOURCES:

Blooms Taxonomy.

https://thesecondprinciple.com/teaching-essentials/beyond-bloom-cognitive-taxonomy-revised/

Dale Carnegie Inc. https://www.dalecarnegie.com/en

Foundation for Critical Thinking https://www.criticalthinking.org/

KIM NUGENT, ED.D.

Self-Assessment Questions

Date: _____ **Week:** _____

Learning goals:

Q: How is problem-solving related to asking questions?
Response:

Q: Have you ever thought about the types of questions you ask?
Response:

Q: Does your school or job have a questioning model they use?
Response:

Q: Research 3 questioning resources. It can be online, book, podcast or TedTalk. Be ready to discuss.
Response:
a).
b).
c).

PAVING YOUR PATH: WHAT'S NEXT FOR HIGH SCHOOL GRADUATES

Q: How will you know you are improving your questioning ability?
Response:

Q: What is one area that you can work on for yourself?
Response:

Q: How will you know you are making progress?
Response:

Q: Journal any extra thoughts, questions, or concerns.
Response:

KIM NUGENT, ED.D.

Mentor Questions

Date: _____ **Week:** _____

This session objectives:

Q: It seems that problem-solving and asking questions are related. Explain to me the relationship and how it can enhance your personal traits.
Response:

Q: What is critical thinking?
Response:

Q: Tell me in your own words how asking questions supports critical thinking?
Response:

Q: Have you ever thought about the type of questions you ask?
Response:

PAVING YOUR PATH: WHAT'S NEXT FOR HIGH SCHOOL GRADUATES

Q: What did you find when you researched three questioning resources? Let's discuss.

Response:

Q: How will you know you are improving your questioning ability?

Response:

Q: How can you help your friends and team members become better at asking questions rather than jumping to conclusions or voicing their opinions?

Response:

Q: Compare and contrast two people you know and their critical thinking ability.

Response:

Q: Create a plan for continuing to develop your critical thinking skills.
Response:

Q: What is one action you can take to improve in this area?
Response:

Q: How will you measure your improvement in this area?
Response:

Q: How can I support you?
Response:

PAVING YOUR PATH: WHAT'S NEXT FOR HIGH SCHOOL GRADUATES

Summary of key observations from today's session:

Q: What went well during the mentoring session?

Q: Were there any challenges during the session?

Q: Next action steps:

RESPONSIBILITY

"You cannot escape the responsibility of tomorrow by evading it today.
—Abraham Lincoln, 16th U.S. President, American lawyer and politician

R IS FOR RESPONSIBILITY

So, who are you in the area of responsibility? Are you naturally responsible at school, work, for your family, and/or for your community? Or do you shy away from responsibility because it seems hard or demanding?

Responsibility is defined as being accountable; taking action on your own or taking the opportunity to act independently. Being responsible is one way to stand out in front of your boss, so you get noticed. What are the actual steps to taking on more responsibility? Alex Cavoulous, President and Founder of The Muse, wrote an excellent article titled *5 Ways to Take on More Responsibility at Work.* First, let's assume you are good at your current role at work.

In your next coaching meeting, talk with your boss about the knowledge and skills you want to develop further. Look for opportunities to help team members. Decide what areas in which you want to become an expert. Be the person everyone in the company goes to because you stay on top of developments and trends. Alex Cavoulus suggests setting up a Google alert for topics relevant to what you are interested in whether personal, school related or professional (p. 3). You get daily email updates this way. I have done this myself and find it a huge time-saver.

One of the traits I look for in developing high-potential employees is the one who takes the initiative; the employee that brings me new ideas or solutions. Someone who is proactive rather than waiting to be told what to do next. For me, the employee that waits to be told what to do is marginal. In this fast-paced world, we cannot accept marginal or just doing your job. Demonstrate your leadership skills. You do not need a title to demonstrate you have what it takes to become an exceptional leader.

Are you the person at work who blames others for your mistakes, your situation, the economy or society? Do you find fault with teachers, band directors, managers? Do you blame others for you not getting what you want? Are you playing the victim, or are you taking personal responsibility for having good grades, a good job, good relationships, and good life? Who are you in this responsibility scenario?

Ron Haskins wrote an article for Brookings Institute called the *Sequence of Personal Responsibility*. Check out this article at https://www.brookings.edu/articles/the-sequence-of-personal-responsibility/

RESOURCES:

5 Ways to Take on More Responsibility at Work by A. Cavoulous.

Google alerts: How to set up https://support.google.com/websearch/

answer/4815696?hl=en

Sequence of Personal Responsibility by R. Haskins. Retrieved from https://www.brookings.edu/articles/the-sequence-of-personal-responsibility/

KIM NUGENT, ED.D.

Self-Assessment Questions

Date: _____   Week: _____

Learning goals:

Q: What does the quote by President Abraham Lincoln at the beginning of this section mean to you?
Response:

Q: What is one area in your life where you can take on personal responsibility?
Response:

Q: What skills and knowledge do you want to develop next?
Response:

Q: Do you see opportunities to help a family member, friend or team member who may be overworked? What are they? Be ready to discuss.
Response:

Q: Where do you find yourself blaming others?
Response:

Q: Have you set up a daily Google© alert to get started? On what topic(s)?
Response:

Q: Taking the initiative is critical to the promotion pathway. If you took a self-assessment, would you consider yourself average or a high-potential employee? What initiative have you taken or could seek to change the situation?
Response:

Q: What is one area that you can work on for yourself?
Response:

Q: How will you know you are making progress?
Response:

Q: Journal any extra thoughts, questions, or concerns.
Response:

PAVING YOUR PATH: WHAT'S NEXT FOR HIGH SCHOOL GRADUATES

"In the long run, we shape our lives, and we shape ourselves. The process never ends until we die. And the choices we make are ultimately our own responsibility.
—Anna Eleanor Roosevelt, American political figure, diplomat and activist, and the longest serving First Lady of the United States.

KIM NUGENT, ED.D.

Mentor Questions

Date: _____   **Week:** _____

This session objectives:

Q: "You cannot escape the responsibility of tomorrow by evading it today." — Abraham Lincoln. What does this quote mean to you?
Response:

Q: What is one area in your life where you can take on personal responsibility?
Response:

Q: What skills and knowledge do you want to develop next?
Response:

Q: What do you think senior managers value in high-potential employees?
Response:

PAVING YOUR PATH: WHAT'S NEXT FOR HIGH SCHOOL GRADUATES

Q: Do you see opportunities to help a family member, friend or team member who may be overworked?

Response:

Q: In what area do you find yourself blaming others?

Response:

Q: Have you set up a daily Google© alert to get started? On what topic(s)?

Response:

Q: How can you develop taking the initiative?

Response:

Q: What is one action you can take to improve in this area?
Response:

Q: How will you measure your improvement in this area?
Response:

Q: How can I support you?
Response:

Summary of key observations from today's session:

Q: What went well during the mentoring session?

Q: Were there any challenges during the session?

Q: Next action steps:

" You must take personal responsibility. You cannot change the circumstances, the seasons, or the wind, but you can change yourself. That is something you have charge of.

—Jim Rohn, American entrepreneur, author and motivational speaker

SELF-AWARENESS

❝ Knowing yourself is key to all wisdom.

—Aristotle, Ancient Greek philosopher.

S IS FOR SELF-AWARENESS

Self-awareness is key to your success. If you know yourself, you get it. Have you looked in the mirror lately? How self-aware are you? Do you know where your blind spots are? Can you identify your strengths? Do you know your weaknesses? If you want to improve your self-awareness, here are some approaches.

You might want to consider conducting your own personal 360° assessment. Find three to six people, who you trust to give you honest feedback, but who are not friends who will just tell you what you want to hear. Ask them the following questions:

(1) Name three of your strength areas. (2) Two areas that need to be developed. (3) One thing they find frustrating about you. (4) What they wish for you? (5) What is an area of expertise for you? (6) What are your blind spots? (7) How you can improve and challenge yourself?

You will be amazed at what you learn about yourself.

There are commercially sold 360° performance assessments that can help. Have you taken any online self-awareness assessments such as Birkman, Myers-Briggs™, DISC™, StrengthsFinder™, Enneagram™,

PathwayU, emotional intelligence, learning styles, career and leadership assessments? What did you learn?

I recently asked a few professional friends what they think their managers think of them, such as, how do you think your teachers or managers think you present yourself? How would they describe your personality traits and leadership style? Tone? Nonverbal expressions? Time-management ability? Team player? Problem-Solver? Respectful? Contributor? Communication style, personality, etc.?

They said they had no idea. Not knowing is a huge problem. If you do not know what people around you are thinking, how will you ever be able to improve?

RESOURCES:

What resources can you bring to this strategy? For example: Books, articles, online resources, or programs.

_____
_____
_____
_____
_____
_____
_____

PAVING YOUR PATH: WHAT'S NEXT FOR HIGH SCHOOL GRADUATES

Self-Assessment Questions

Date: _____   Week: _____

Learning goals:

Q: What did you learn from the interviews you conducted?
Response:

Q: What are three of your strength areas?
Response:

Q: What are two areas that need to be developed?
Response:

Q: What is one thing they find frustrating about you?
Response:

PAVING YOUR PATH: WHAT'S NEXT FOR HIGH SCHOOL GRADUATES

Q: What do they wish for you?

Response:

Q: What is an area where you excel?

Response:

Q: What are your blind spots?

Response:

Q: How can you improve and challenge yourself?

Response:

Q: What is one area that you can work on for yourself?
Response:

Q: How will you know you are making progress?
Response:

Q: Journal any extra thoughts, questions, or concerns.
Response:

"The person we believe ourselves to be will always act in a manner consistent with our self-image.
—Brian Tracy, American author, entrepreneur and motivational speaker

Mentor Questions

Date: _____   **Week:** _____

This session objectives:

Q: Based on the interviews you conducted what did you learn?

Response:

Q: Based on the interviews you conducted what surprised you?

Response:

Q: Have you taken any online self-awareness assessments? If yes, what did you learn or confirm?

Response:

Q: Have you ever taken any personal-development courses to discover your blind spots? If so, what classes? What did you find out?

Response:

PAVING YOUR PATH: WHAT'S NEXT FOR HIGH SCHOOL GRADUATES

Q: What traits are essential to leadership or promotability?
Response:

Q: How can I support you in your quest for self-assessment?
Response:

Q: What is one action you can take to improve in this area?
Response:

Q: How will you measure your improvement in this area?
Response:

Q: How can I further support you?
Response:

Summary of key observations from today's session:

Q: What went well during the mentoring session?

Q: Were there any challenges during the session?

Q: Next action steps:

"Authenticity means erasing the gap between what you firmly believe inside and what you reveal to the outside world.
—Adam Grant, American psychologist, author, and professor of organizational psychology

THANK YOU

> " Make it a habit of telling people thank you. To express your appreciation, sincerely and without the expectation of anything in return. Truly appreciate those around you, and you'll soon find many others around you. Truly appreciate life, and honestly, you will find you have more of it.
> —Ralph Marston, The Daily Motivator

T IS FOR THANK YOU

When was the last time you said, "Thank you?" Those two words are some of the most important words for your career and your life. When was the last time you wrote a handwritten "Thank you" note? Not an email or a tweet but a real handwritten note. You might think this is old school, but the impression you make by doing this speaks volumes. The fact that you are taking the time to acknowledge someone means a great deal.

Think about opportunities to say thank you. Did your mentor give you some solid advice? Did you seek a job recommendation? Did someone help you with a letter of recommendation? Did you go out on a job interview? Did you write a follow-up thank you? Were you given a job? Did you say thank you? Were you given a promotion? Did you say thank you? Did you thank your team members when they completed a project on time? Were you given a bonus? Did you say thank you? You might be thinking, "Hey I earned it...what's the big deal?" That attitude is an entitlement attitude. How about being grateful and saying "thank you" instead? When was the last time you said thank you to a family member?

Did a co-worker take the time to help you out? Did someone remember your birthday or work anniversary? Did someone take you to coffee, lunch, or dinner and they paid?

Did you attend a company dinner or event? Did you thank the host? Did you say, "thank you"? Did someone drive you to a meeting? Did you say thank you? When was the last time you thanked your boss?

As you can see from the above examples, there are ample opportunities to say thank you. If this is not your strong suit, schedule a reminder on your calendar to do this weekly at a minimum. Try it and see what happens! Make this a habit each week.

RESOURCES:

What resources can you bring to this strategy? For example: Books, articles, online resources, or programs.

_____

_____

_____

_____

_____

_____

PAVING YOUR PATH: WHAT'S NEXT FOR HIGH SCHOOL GRADUATES

KIM NUGENT, ED.D.

Self-Assessment Questions

Date: _____   **Week:** _____

Learning goals:

••
Q: Where have you noticed opportunities to say thank you?
Response:

••
Q: Have you noticed missed opportunities to say thank you?
Response:

••
Q: How does it make you feel when you say or write a thank you note?
Response:

••
Q: Does this come naturally?
Response:

PAVING YOUR PATH: WHAT'S NEXT FOR HIGH SCHOOL GRADUATES

Q: Do you need to schedule a reminder on your calendar?
Response:

Q: How important in life and business do you think it is to say thank you?
Response:

Q: What is one area that you can work on for yourself?
Response:

Q: How will you know you are making progress?
Response:

Q: Journal any extra thoughts, questions, or concerns.
Response:

KIM NUGENT, ED.D.

Mentor Questions

Date: _____   Week: _____

This session objectives:

Q: There is a statement that is often quoted that "employees do not quit organizations, they quit people." What does this mean to you?
Response:

Q: What kind of person, employee, or leader do you want to be?
Response:

Q: How important is it that employees and team members feel appreciated?
Response:

Q: What makes you feel appreciated?
Response:

PAVING YOUR PATH: WHAT'S NEXT FOR HIGH SCHOOL GRADUATES

Q: Where have you noticed opportunities to say thank you?
Response:

Q: Have you noticed missed opportunities to say thank you?
Response:

Q: How important in business do you think it is to say thank you?
Response:

Q: How can I further support you in developing your "thank-you" muscle?
Response:

Q: What is one action you can take to improve in this area?
Response:

Q: How will you measure your improvement in this area?
Response:

Q: How can I support you?
Response:

Summary of key observations from today's session:

Q: What went well during the mentoring session?

Q: Were there any challenges during the session?

Q: Next action steps:

"Be thankful for what you have; you'll end up having more. If you concentrate on what you don't have, you will never, ever have enough.

—Oprah Winfrey, American media executive, actress, talk show host, television producer and philanthropist.

UNIQUE

> "A human being is a single being. Unique and unrepeatable.
> —Eileen Caddy, Spiritual teacher

U IS FOR UNIQUE

You are unique and talented so try not to compare yourself to others. This is true at work, at play, and in life. I enjoy taking hot yoga classes. I love the way it makes me feel. The teachers are always reminding us not to compare our practice to others. Every person comes to yoga each day. Some days the postures are natural. Some days the poses are more challenging. Regardless, I am mindful of my self-talk. It is always positive. I made a point of going to yoga and giving myself the gift of an hour. I do not look around and compare myself to new practitioners or experienced practitioners. After all, it is my practice.

I believe this is also true at work; your uniqueness can be fully expressed through your authenticity. You are real, genuine, and one-of-a-kind. Positively capitalize on your uniqueness. Be engaging, fresh, current, and relevant. Being unique is not being or feeling superior. The Yoga One studio owner, Roger Rippy, and author of the *Love Revolution* shared his very own story about this when he grew up. He said, "You have to run your own race." He added, "The question is how you acknowledge, appreciate, develop what your uniqueness is, and what you have."

- Where are you exceptional?

- What do you love doing?

- What do you enjoy?

- How can you serve others?

- What inspires you?

RESOURCES:

What resources can you bring to this strategy? For example: Books, articles, online resources, or programs.

_____

_____

_____

_____

_____

_____

_____

PAVING YOUR PATH: WHAT'S NEXT FOR HIGH SCHOOL GRADUATES

KIM NUGENT, ED.D.

Self-Assessment Questions

Date: _____ **Week:** _____

Learning goals:

Q: Where are you exceptional?
Response:

Q: What do you love doing?
Response:

Q: What do you enjoy?
Response:

Q: How can you serve others?
Response:

PAVING YOUR PATH: WHAT'S NEXT FOR HIGH SCHOOL GRADUATES

Q: What inspires you?
Response:

Q: What is one area that you can work on for yourself?
Response:

Q: How will you know you are making progress?
Response:

Q: Journal any extra thoughts, questions, or concerns.
Response:

Mentor Questions

Date: _____   **Week:** _____

This session objectives:

Q: Each and every person is unique. Where are you exceptional? How does that serve you?
Response:

Q: What do you love doing?
Response:

Q: Who does it serve?
Response:

Q: How can you share this with others?
Response:

PAVING YOUR PATH: WHAT'S NEXT FOR HIGH SCHOOL GRADUATES

Q: What do you enjoy? How can you share with others to better serve them?
Response:

Q: What inspires you? How can you use your inspiration to serve others?
Response:

Q: What have you always wanted to do? How can that serve others?
Response:

Q: What is one action you can take to improve in this area?
Response:

Q: How will you measure your improvement in this area?

Response:

Q: How can I support you?

Response:

Summary of key observations from today's session:

Q: What went well during the mentoring session?

Q: Were there any challenges during the session?

Q: Next action steps:

"Show off your own style and uniqueness to stand out. That's the advice I'd give to people getting started online now.

—Conor Maynard, English singer-songwriter, record producer, and actor

VISION

> " The visionary starts with a clean sheet of paper and reimagines the world.
> —Malcolm Gladwell, Canadian journalist, author and public speaker

V IS FOR VISION

What vision do you have for your life? Visualize what you want for yourself. What do you love doing? What type of career? What job roles? What salary do you want to earn? What do you want for financial security? What educational level do you want to attain? Where do you want to live? What do you want your relationships to look like? What hobbies do you enjoy? Do you have a spiritual practice? Do you want to bring creativity into your life?

Who do you see yourself becoming? How does it feel? What do you see? Make a mental picture. Write it down. Create a vision board on a poster board or paper that inspires you, motivates, brings you joy. Use pictures and colors. Be specific. Place it where you see it every day. There is scientific evidence to support the power of visualization. What you focus on, you achieve.

What are people saying about you? The more you can bring all your senses into this vision you have for yourself, the more likely you will achieve it. Write it down. Look at it every day. Repeat it as an affirmation. Write down the goals you want to achieve. Do you believe it is possible? If yes, great. Get yourself out of the way and make it happen.

You are more likely to achieve the life you want, if you write your goals down and revisit them daily.

As an emerging leader, it is imperative that you have a vision of where you want to take the organization, department, or team. The more that you can paint the picture for them, the more likely you will achieve it. When you are storytelling about the vision, bring in all senses.

One of my former bosses asked us to engage in this great exercise. He would describe the project we were working on in detail. He would then ask us to close our eyes and think about three years from now. He would say "Let's pretend we are at a company picnic celebrating our success. What would we have accomplished? What were people saying about the organization internally and externally? How did you feel? What was the day like? What sounds could you hear? What did you see around you?" By the time we finished the exercise, everyone could see in their own mind's eye where we were going and how we would feel when we got there. It is truly inspiring! At subsequent meetings, he would remind us of the picture of the picnic so we would not lose sight of where we were going and what we could accomplish.

How can you use the picnic exercise for your life? What will it look like in three years? Where will you be? What will you be doing? Who will you surround yourself with? How will you feel? Good luck!

RESOURCES:

What resources can you bring to this strategy? For example: Books, articles, online resources, or programs.

_____
_____
_____
_____
_____
_____
_____
_____

KIM NUGENT, ED.D.

Self-Assessment Questions

Date: _____   **Week:** _____

Learning goals:

Q: What do you want for yourself and your life?
Response:

Q: What type of career do you envision? What job roles? What salary do you want to earn?
Response:

Q: What do you want for financial security?
Response:

Q: What educational level do you want to attain?
Response:

PAVING YOUR PATH: WHAT'S NEXT FOR HIGH SCHOOL GRADUATES

Q: Where do you want to live?
Response:

Q: What do you want your relationships to look like?
Response:

Q: What hobbies do you enjoy?
Response:

Q: What about spirituality or creativity?
Response:

Q: Who do you see yourself becoming? How does it feel? What do you see? Write it down. Create a vision board. Create a board that inspires you, motivates, and brings you joy. Place it someplace where you see it every day.
Response:

Q: What is one area that you can work on for yourself?
Response:

Q: How will you know you are making progress?
Response:

Q: Journal any extra thoughts, questions, or concerns.
Response:

PAVING YOUR PATH: WHAT'S NEXT FOR HIGH SCHOOL GRADUATES

"The path from dreams to success does exist. May you have the vision to find it, the courage to get on to it, and the perseverance to follow it.

—Kalpana Chawla, American astronaut

KIM NUGENT, ED.D.

Mentor Questions

Date: _____   **Week:** _____

This session objectives:

Q: It is imperative that you have a vision of where you want to take your life. How would you describe the picture?
Response:

Q: What is the story of your life?
Response:

Q: Could you lead the picnic exercise as described? How would you bring in all the senses? Share your version of this exercise with me.
Response:

Q: What is one action you can take to improve in this area?
Response:

PAVING YOUR PATH: WHAT'S NEXT FOR HIGH SCHOOL GRADUATES

Q: How will you measure your improvement in this area?
Response:

Q: How can I support you?
Response:

Summary of key observations from today's session:

Q: What went well during the mentoring session?

Q: Were there any challenges during the session?

Q: Next action steps:

WHITE LIES

" White lies always introduce others of a darker complexion.

—William S. Paley, Chief Executive CBS

W IS FOR WHITE LIES

I am often surprised at how people tell white lies. They feel justified for whatever reason. Example: "I am going to take home office supplies. It is no big deal. The company can afford it." Would you feel the same way if you owned the company?

Years ago, I took over a company that was in desperate financial trouble. I was uncertain for a time whether we would meet payroll every other week. I needed the employees to understand the situation without causing panic. So, I had a little fun with it. I asked them to all return our special signature pens the next day. I called it "Amnesty Day." I was looking for a thousand ways to reduce expenses while not losing sight of all the details. The next day the employees brought back over 1,000 custom signature pens. Have I made my point?

For the employees, it seemed like no big deal, but it was indeed a symbol for all of us to work together and turn the situation around, and we did. You might feel someone mistreated you, you deserve something, and you justify it. The truth is that white lies become bigger lies. Over time, people forget what the truth is. Lying has a way of holding you hostage. You can justify all you want, but it costs you. It costs you integrity, relationships, jobs, freedom, and authenticity.

A second example is when you tell your teacher, parent or supervisor the report is done but it isn't. You built in time to turn it in on time, but you actually lied about the present state of the report.

Another example is in social media. How truthful do you think you are in the way you present yourself in social media? Your photo? Your resume? Your relationships? Your reputation? Is it the truth or a lie? Be careful: big brother and your employer are always watching.

RESOURCES:

What resources can you bring to this strategy? For example: Books, articles, online resources, or programs.

_____
_____
_____
_____
_____
_____
_____

PAVING YOUR PATH: WHAT'S NEXT FOR HIGH SCHOOL GRADUATES

KIM NUGENT, ED.D.

Self-Assessment Questions

Date: _____   Week: _____

Learning goals:

Q: Where have you told white lies?
Response:

Q: How did you justify it?
Response:

Q: What did it cost you? Or what could it cost you?
Response:

Q: Do you ever think white lies become more significant over time?
Response:

PAVING YOUR PATH: WHAT'S NEXT FOR HIGH SCHOOL GRADUATES

Q: What is one area that you can work on for yourself?
Response:

Q: How will you know you are making progress?
Response:

Q: Journal any extra thoughts, questions, or concerns.
Response:

Mentor Questions

Date: _____   **Week:** _____

This session objectives:

Q: What did you think about "Amnesty Day" and the returned pens?
Response:

Q: Do you think most people feel justified in telling white lies? What do you think the point of it is?
Response:

Q: Do you think there is ever a time when a white lie is justified?
Response:

Q: As a future leader, how can you create a culture of truth and integrity?
Response:

PAVING YOUR PATH: WHAT'S NEXT FOR HIGH SCHOOL GRADUATES

Q: How do you model transparency?
Response:

Q: What is one action you can take to improve in this area?
Response:

Q: How will you measure your improvement in this area?
Response:

Q: How can I support you?
Response:

Summary of key observations from today's session:

Q: What went well during the mentoring session?

Q: Were there any challenges during the session?

Q: Next action steps:

PAVING YOUR PATH: WHAT'S NEXT FOR HIGH SCHOOL GRADUATES

"A lack of transparency results in distrust and a deep sense of insecurity.

–Dalai Lama, Buddhist monk and spiritual teacher

X-FACTOR

" The X-Factor saved me.
—James Arthur, English singer and songwriter

X IS FOR X-FACTOR

I believe exceptional leaders have the X-Factor. The traits for exceptional leaders are distinct from general leadership traits. I think most people cannot describe the traits of an exceptional leader, as they have not had the experience of working for one. Based on my experience, I created the following traits that I believe exist in exceptional leaders as follows:

Authentic: Genuine, real, transparent, and comfortable with who they are.

Depth: Understand the organization across all boundaries and themselves; willing to try new things; take risks.

Eclectic: Come to the position with a varied background of experiences; unique.

Energy of Being: Energy level has what it takes in good times and in bad; resilient.

Generosity of Spirit: The ability to connect and relate to human beings; heart-centered; culturally sensitive.

Texture: Brings a sense of creativity when approaching each situation; multi-dimensional.

Visionary: Able to plan for the future and inspire others to achieve the vision, mission, and goals.

So, what is your X-Factor? What is your unique talent? How can you positively impact the outcome of your life?

Can you relate to any of the exceptional leadership traits? Are you authentic? Creative? Eclectic? Have depth? Do you have a variety of experiences? Do you have a presence? Do you have texture? Do you have credibility? Are you innovative? Do you have a generosity of spirit? Are you interesting? Are you visionary? How many of these talents do you possess? Given your assessment, would you want to promote yourself? Be truthful.

RESOURCES:

What resources can you bring to this strategy? For example: Books, articles, online resources, or programs.

_____
_____
_____
_____
_____
_____
_____

KIM NUGENT, ED.D.

Self-Assessment Questions

Date: _____   **Week:** _____

Learning goals:

Q: What is your X-Factor?
Response:

Q: What is your unique talent?
Response:

Q: How can you positively impact people around you at work or school?
Response:

Q: Can you relate to any of the seven exceptional leadership traits?
Response:
1). Authentic   6). Texture
2). Depth   7). Visionary
3). Eclectic
4). Energy of Being
5) Generosity of Spirit

PAVING YOUR PATH: WHAT'S NEXT FOR HIGH SCHOOL GRADUATES

Q: How many of these talents do you possess?
Response:

Q: Given your assessment, would you want to promote you?
Response:

Q: What is one area that you can work on for yourself?
Response:

Q: How will you know you are making progress?
Response:

Q: Journal any extra thoughts, questions, or concerns.
Response:

KIM NUGENT, ED.D.

Mentor Questions

Date: _____   **Week:** _____

This session objectives:

Q: Let's discuss each of these seven traits of an exceptional leader. What does it mean to be Authentic?
Response:

Q: What does it mean to have Depth?
Response:

Q: What does it mean to be Eclectic? What experiences do you bring?
Response:

Q: What is your Energy level? How resilient are you in bad times? Give me an example.
Response:

PAVING YOUR PATH: WHAT'S NEXT FOR HIGH SCHOOL GRADUATES

Q: Do you feel you have a Generosity of Spirit? Do you think you have the ability to connect and relate to human beings?

Response:

Q: Do you have Texture? Do you have the ability to bring a sense of creativity when approaching each situation? Give me an example.

Response:

Q: Do you feel that one day you will have the ability to be a Visionary? Do you think you have the ability to inspire others to achieve the vision, mission, and goals? Give me an example.

Response:

Q: What is one action you can take to improve in this area?

Response:

Q: How will you measure your improvement in this area?
Response:

Q: How can I support you?
Response:

Summary of key observations from today's session:

Q: What went well during the mentoring session?

Q: Were there any challenges during the session?

Q: Next action steps:

"Be a warrior when it comes to delivering on your ambitions. And a saint when it comes to treating people with respect, modeling generosity, and showing up with outright love.
—Robin Sharma, Canadian author, speaker, entrepreneur and litigation lawyer.

YEARNING

> "There are three ingredients for a good life: learning, earning, and yearning.
> —Christopher Morley, Artist and designer

Y IS FOR YEARNING

Do you have an innate yearning to become a better you? Do you have a zest for life? Do you have a love for learning? Do you yearn to earn? Do you yearn to travel and experience new things? This is not to say you are not satisfied but rather have energy that encompasses the essence of your being. Yearning is not related to age. Yearning can exist at any age.

Yearning is defined as a strong desire to have or intense longing for something.

I had a yearning to teach at the college level and share my professional experiences and mentor others professionally. This is distinct from coaching. I had the academic credentials. I had the business experience and proven track record, but I did not have the tools to deliver an engaging classroom experience at the beginning of my new career path. The yearning was incredible and yet I knew I had to go to work and learn as much as I could if I was going to master the art and science of teaching. I attribute that yearning to carrying me through those hard and difficult times when I wanted to give up and persevered so I could obtain personal and professional mastery. I truly believe all things are possible with a yearning, effort, and persistence.

Explore your possibilities. Explore your values. Explore your beliefs. What do you yearn for in your life? Be specific and go for it!

RESOURCES:

What resources can you bring to this strategy? For example: Books, articles, online resources, or programs.

_____
_____
_____
_____
_____
_____

PAVING YOUR PATH: WHAT'S NEXT FOR HIGH SCHOOL GRADUATES

KIM NUGENT, ED.D.

Self-Assessment Questions

Date: _____   Week: _____

Learning goals:

Q: What do you yearn for beyond high school?
Response:

Q: Where do you start to make this happen?
Response:

Q: What could stop you?
Response:

Q: What is your timeline?
Response:

PAVING YOUR PATH: WHAT'S NEXT FOR HIGH SCHOOL GRADUATES

Q: What is one area that you can work on for yourself?
Response:

Q: How will you know you are making progress?
Response:

Q: Journal any extra thoughts, questions, or concerns.
Response:

KIM NUGENT, ED.D.

Mentor Questions

Date: _____   **Week:** _____

This session objectives:

- -
Q: What do you yearn for beyond high school?
Response:

- -
Q: Where do you start to make this happen?
Response:

- -
Q: What could stop you?
Response:

- -
Q: What is your timeline?
Response:

PAVING YOUR PATH: WHAT'S NEXT FOR HIGH SCHOOL GRADUATES

Q: What is one action you can take to improve in this area?
Response:

Q: How will you measure your improvement in this area?
Response:

Q: How can I support you?
Response:

Summary of key observations from today's session:

Q: What went well during the mentoring session?

Q: Were there any challenges during the session?

Q: Next action steps:

ZONE

> "The miracle often lies outside our comfort zone.
> —Marianne Williamson, American spiritual teacher

Z IS FOR ZONE

I have often heard athletes describe being in the zone when everything they do seems to be going in the right direction. I am sure you have your favorite stories and examples of this so you can imagine what being in the zone must feel like.

Being in the zone is described as being in the flow or flow state. Think back to a time when you lost track of time because you were in flow or the zone. Now that we have come to trait Z, number 26, do you feel you are in the zone? Have you ever been in the zone? What does it feel like? What were you doing? Describe the sensations.

If you are not in the zone now, how can you get back there? What is your energy level? What goals have you set? What actions are you taking? There is a great article written by Sarah Chang on *The Best Tricks for Getting in the Zone at Work*. It can be retrieved at https://www.themuse.com/advice/the-best-tricks-for-getting-in-the-zone-at-work. She describes tools to get back into the flow state. What project can you be working on that challenges you? What goals do you want to accomplish? Can you create a space with little or few interruptions?

What are you not doing that you need to be doing? What should you keep doing that works? What should you stop doing? Are you committed to getting back to being in the zone state and take it to the next level? Turn off the TV and get started!

RESOURCES:

The Best Tricks for Getting in the Zone at Work by S. Chang. Retrieved from https://www.themuse.com/advice/the-best-tricks-for-getting-in-the-zone-at-work

PAVING YOUR PATH: WHAT'S NEXT FOR HIGH SCHOOL GRADUATES

KIM NUGENT, ED.D.

Self-Assessment Questions

Date: _____ **Week:** _____

Learning goals:

Q: Do you know how to get yourself in the zone?
Response:

Q: Describe when you were in the zone and how it felt.
Response:

Q: Do you know what helps you stay in the zone?
Response:

Q: Read the article by Sarah Chang and check out the resources.
Response:

PAVING YOUR PATH: WHAT'S NEXT FOR HIGH SCHOOL GRADUATES

Q: Final Reflection: Write out what you believe you have accomplished through "Paving Your Path" process. Be prepared to discuss.

Response:

Mentor Questions

Date: _____   **Week:** _____

This session objectives:

Q: What did you think about being in the zone? Do you know how to get yourself in the zone?
Response:

Q: After reading the article by Sarah Chang what do you think?
Response:

Q: How can you help your team get in the zone?
Response:

Q: How can I support you?
Response:

PAVING YOUR PATH: WHAT'S NEXT FOR HIGH SCHOOL GRADUATES

Q: Final Reflection: Now that you have completed "Paving Your Path" program, what do you believe you have accomplished? Complete the self-awareness inventory again to chart your progress.

Response:

Q: What have you learned?

Response:

Q: How have you changed?

Response:

KIM NUGENT, ED.D.

SELF-ASSESSMENT INVENTORY: POST ASSESSMENT

CHAPTER 8

ABC's of Possibilities	Plan to improve/Resources utilized
Rate Yourself 1 – 10. 1 being poor and 10 being excellent.	
1 2 3 4 5 6 7 8 9 10 Attitude: What is your attitude?	
1 2 3 4 5 6 7 8 9 10 Brand: How are you known? What impression do you make face-to-face or through social media?	
1 2 3 4 5 6 7 8 9 10 Communication: How effective are your communications skills?	

ABC's of Possibilities	Plan to improve/Resources utilized
Rate Yourself 1 – 10. 1 being poor and 10 being excellent.	
1 2 3 4 5 6 7 8 9 10 Depth: What is your personal depth? What do you know?	
1 2 3 4 5 6 7 8 9 10 Emotional Intelligence: What is your emotional intelligence quotient?	
1 2 3 4 5 6 7 8 9 10 Focused: How focused are you?	
1 2 3 4 5 6 7 8 9 10 Gratitude: How grateful are you?	
1 2 3 4 5 6 7 8 9 10 Habits: How effective are your habits?	
1 2 3 4 5 6 7 8 9 10 Integrity: How well do you keep your word to yourself and others?	

ABC's of Possibilities	Plan to improve/Resources utilized
Rate Yourself 1 – 10. 1 being poor and 10 being excellent.	
1 2 3 4 5 6 7 8 9 10 Jaded: Are there areas in your life where you feel jaded?	
1 2 3 4 5 6 7 8 9 10 Knowledgeable: How knowledgeable are you?	
1 2 3 4 5 6 7 8 9 10 Life-Long Learning: How committed are you to life-long learning?	
1 2 3 4 5 6 7 8 9 10 Mindset: Do you have a growth- or fixed-mindset?	
1 2 3 4 5 6 7 8 9 10 Network: How strong is your social network?	
1 2 3 4 5 6 7 8 9 10 Opportunity: Do you see life as an opportunity?	

ABC's of Possibilities	Plan to improve/Resources utilized
Rate Yourself 1 – 10. 1 being poor and 10 being excellent.	
1 2 3 4 5 6 7 8 9 10 Problem-Solver: How effective are your problem-solving skills? Do you tend to be logical and have a process or are you emotional?	
1 2 3 4 5 6 7 8 9 10 Question: How effective are your questioning skills?	
1 2 3 4 5 6 7 8 9 10 Responsibility: How strong is your sense of responsibility?	
1 2 3 4 5 6 7 8 9 10 Self-Awareness: How self-aware are you?	
1 2 3 4 5 6 7 8 9 10 Thank You: How appreciative are you? Do you always say thank you?	

ABC's of Possibilities	Plan to improve/Resources utilized
Rate Yourself 1 – 10. 1 being poor and 10 being excellent.	
1 2 3 4 5 6 7 8 9 10 Unique: How unique are you?	
1 2 3 4 5 6 7 8 9 10 Vision: Have you created a vision for your life?	
1 2 3 4 5 6 7 8 9 10 White-Lies: Do you find yourself telling white-lies and justifying them?	
1 2 3 4 5 6 7 8 9 10 X-Factor: What is the X-factor you bring?	
1 2 3 4 5 6 7 8 9 10 Yearning: Do you have a real yearning for life?	
1 2 3 4 5 6 7 8 9 10 Zone: Do you feel you are in the zone?	

"Success is a journey, not a destination. The doing is often more important than the outcome.
—Arthur Ashe, American athlete

THE FINAL MENTOR-MENTEE MEETING

WEEK 30:

Review of all deliverables for your chosen pathway. Celebrate. What is next for you?

I am sure you have both grown through this process and strengthened the relationship. Soon you will be graduating from high school. Be grateful for the journey with your mentor. You are both changed as a result of this experience.

CONGRATULATIONS!

Thank each other for the experience.

KIM NUGENT, ED.D.

ONLINE RESOURCES
CHAPTER 11

Eight Steps to Filling Out FAFSA:

https://blog.ed.gov/2017/09/8-steps-to-filling-out-the-fafsa-form/

FAFSA Financial Aid Tutorial:

https://www.edvisors.com/fafsa/forms/tutorial/

Mind Mapping

https://www.mindmeister.com/?utm_source=google&utm_medium=cpc&utm_campaign=us_en_search&utm_content=mm&gclid=C-j0KCQiAzKnjBRDPARIsAKxfTRBjRalyOrZUEBb-K5UFjoj4x7tskahgk66YfnYOSiYIop88K1Xy2owaAumrEALw_wcB

Study Skills for High School Students:

https://cws.auburn.edu/shared/content/files/50/WISE_Study_Tips.pdf

Teaching Study Skills:

https://study.com/academy/lesson/teaching-study-skills-to-high-school-students.html

"It is in your moments of decision that your destiny is shaped.
–Tony Robbins, American author, philanthropist and life coach

REFERENCES

Alton, L. (Sep. 7, 2016). *How sleep deprivation affects your day at the office.* Retrieved from https://www.forbes.com/sites/larryalton/2016/09/07/heres-how-sleep-affects-your-day-at-the-office/#3ed1c8e7820b

AmeriCorps. (2019). *Corporation for national and community service.* Retrieved from https://www.nationalservice.gov/programs/americorps

Anderson. L. & Krathwohl, D. (2001). *Revised Bloom's taxonomy.* Retrieved from https://thesecondprinciple.com/teaching-essentials/beyond-bloom-cognitive-taxonomy-revised/

Attitude. (2018). Retrieved from https://www.google.com/

Beck, R. & Harter, J. (2015). *Managers account for 70% of the variance in employee engagement.* Retrieved from http://news.gallup.com/businessjournal/182792/managers-account-variance-employee-engagement.aspx

Bloom, B. (1956). *Bloom's taxonomy.* Retrieved from http://www.nwlink.com/~donclark/hrd/bloom.html

Brainy Quotes. (n.d.). Retrieved from https://www.brainyquote.com/

Brown, L. & Rohn, J. (2019). *Why attitude is everything.* Retrieved from https://www.youtube.com/watch?v=nbfFDnKkMvw

Bungay, G. (Jul 13, 2015). *Remarkable employees: The characteristics of high potentials.* Retrieved from http://performancecritical.com/remarkable-employees-characteristics-high-potentials/

Buzan, T. (2019). *Father of mind mapping.* Retrieved from https://www.tonybuzan.com/

Carnegie, D. (2013). *The five essential people skills: How to assert yourself, listen to others, and resolve conflicts.* Retrieved from https://www.youtube.com/watch?v=zvZbeplavY0

Cavoulous, A. (n.d.). *Ways to take on more responsibility at work.* Retrieved from https://www.themuse.com/advice/5-ways-to-take-on-more-responsibility-at-work

Chang, S. (n.d.). *The best tricks for getting in the zone at work.* Retrieved from https://www.themuse.com/advice/the-best-tricks-for-getting-in-the-zone-at-work.

Communication skills: How to improve communication skills 7 tips. (2018). Retrieved from https://www.youtube.com/watch?v=mPRUNGGORDo

Connellan, T. (2002). *Bringing out the best in others! 3 keys for business leaders, educators, coaches, and parents.* Retrieved from https://www.amazon.com/Bringing-Out-Best-Others-Educators/dp/188516758X/ref=sr_1_1?ie=UTF8&qid=1520700987&sr=8-1&keywords=bringing+out+the+best+in+others

Dale Carnegie. (2018). Retrieved from https://www.dalecarnegie.com/en/franchise-locations

Dijulius, J. R. III. (2003). *Secret service: Hidden systems that produce unforgettable customer service.* Retrieved from https://www.amazon.com/Secret-Service-Systems-Unforgettable-Customer/dp/0814471714/ref=sr_1_3?ie=UTF8&qid=1520797468&sr=8-3&keywords=secret+service+book

Dweck, C. (2009). *Mindset: How we can learn to fulfill our potential.* Retrieved from https://www.amazon.com/Mindset-Psychology-Carol-S-Dweck/dp/0345472322/ref=sr_1_1?ie=UTF8&qid=1518884922&sr=8-1&keywords=mindset+by+carol+dweck

Emmons, R. A. (2004). *The psychology of gratitude.* Retrieved from https://www.forbes.com/sites/larryalton/2016/09/07/heres-how-sleep-affects-your-day-at-the-office/#3ed1c8e7820b

Emotional Intelligence. (2018). Retrieved from https://www.youtube.com/watch?v=Y7m9eNoB3NU

FAFSA. (2019). *Federal student aid: Office of the department of education.* Retrieved from https://studentaid.ed.gov/sa/fafsa

Fast Web. (2019). *Find scholarships for free.* Retrieved from https://www.fastweb.com/

Goleman, D. (1995). *Emotional Intelligence: Why it can matter more than IQ.* New York, NY: Bantam Books.

Gordon, J. (2007). *How to deal with energy vampires.* Retrieved from http://www.jongordon.com/positive-tip-energy-vampires

Grammarly. (2018). Retrieved from https://www.grammarly.com

Hogan, R. & Hogan, J. (2001). Assessing leadership: a view of the dark side. *International Journal of Evaluation and Assessment, 9,* 40-51.

Holmes, L. (Dec. 2017). *10 things grateful people do differently.* Retrieved from https://www.huffingtonpost.com/entry/habits-of-grateful-people_us_565352a6e4b0d4093a588538

Kaiser, H. (n.d.). *What is problem-solving?* Retrieved from https://www.mindtools.com/pages/article/newTMC_00.htm

Liotta, A. (2012). *Unlocking generational codes: Understanding what makes the generations tick and what ticks them off.* Retrieved from http://resultance.com/

Management Mentors. (2018). Retrieved from https://www.management-mentors.com/resources/corporate-mentoring-programs-resources-faqs#Q1

Maxwell, J. C. (2003). *Attitude 101: What every leader needs to know.* Retrieved from https://www.amazon.com/Attitude-101-Every-Leader-Needs/dp/0785263500

McKinsey and Co. (May 2000). *Leadership development: Where is the ROI?* Retrieved from www.hri.eckerrd.edu

Mehrabian, A. (1972). *Nonverbal Communication.* Chicago, Il. Aldine-Atherton.

Mehrabian, A. (n.d.). *Communication Model.* Mehrabian Retrieved from https://www.toolshero.com/communication-skills/communication-model-mehrabian/

Mindtools.com. (2018). *Improve your listening skills with active listening.* Retrieved from https://www.youtube.com/watch?v=t2z9mdX1j4A

Moran, G. (2017). *Ditch these seven bad habits before 2018 starts.* Retrieved from https://www.fastcompany.com/40503547/ditch-these-seven-bad-habits-before-2018-starts

Myhre, M. (Nov. 2005). *Developing personal depth.* Retrieved from http://www.articlecity.com/articles/self_improvement_and_motivation/article_3237.shtml

Nalin, J. (May 2017). *7 ways to teach teen's emotional intelligence.* Retrieved from https://paradigmmalibu.com/7-teach-teens-emotional-intelligence/

National Speakers Association. (2018). Retrieved from https://www.nsaspeaker.org/

PathwayU. (2019). *Student success from enrollment to retirement.* Retrieved from https://promotionprotocol.pathwayu.com/login?next=%2Fjourney

Personal Image Presence. (2018). *Professional Image Audit.* Retrieved from https://www.evansville.edu/careercenter/downloads/ProfessionalImageSelfAudit.pdf?v=2

Peters, T. (2004). *The brand called you.* Retrieved from https://www.fastcompany.com/28905/brand-called-you

Reynolds, J. (Mar 1, 2017). *20 characteristics of high-potential employees.* Retrieved from https://www.tinypulse.com/blog/20-characteristics-of-high-potential-employees

Rippy, R. (2017). *Love revolution: A 21-day program to create a life you love.* Retrieved from https://www.facebook.com/events/880164042160109/

Robbins, M. (2018). *Bring your whole self to work.* Retrieved from https://www.youtube.com/watch?v=bd2WKQWG_Dg

Sinek, S. (2011). *Start with why: How great leaders inspire action.* Retrieved from https://www.ted.com/talks/simon_sinek_how_great_leaders_inspire_action

Small Business Administration (SBA). (n. d). Retrieved from https://www.sba.gov/

Small Business Development Center – Houston. (2019). Retrieved from https://www.sbdc.uh.edu/sbdc/default.asp

Social Media Audit Template (2018). Retrieved from https://blog.hootsuite.com/social-media-audit-template/

Student success agency. (2019). *Representing teens to success.* Retrieved from https://studentsuccess.co/

Ted Talks. (2018). Retrieved from https://www.youtube.com/channel/UCAuUUnT6oDeKwE6v1NGQxug

Toastmasters International. (2018). Retrieved from https://www.toastmasters.org/

The Attitude Test. (2019). Retrieved from https://www.3smartcubes.com/pages/tests/attitudetest/attitudetest_instructions/Online attitude assessments

The Foundation for Critical Thinking. (2018). Retrieved from https://www.criticalthinking.org/

The Global Leadership Foundation. (2018). *Emotional Intelligence Test.* Retrieved from https://globalleadershipfoundation.com/geit/eitest.html

TILE. (2019). *Talks on innovation, leadership and entrepreneurship.* Retrieved from https://www.tile.org/.

Unigo. (2019). *College matching and school reviews.* Retrieved from https://www.unigo.com/scholarships/our-scholarships

Wray, M. (2014). *Creating Positive Futures: 6 simple strategies for improving student focus.* Retrieved from http://creatingpositivefutures.com/6-simple-strategies-for-improving-students-focus/

ABOUT THE AUTHOR
KIM NUGENT, ED.D.

Dr. Kim Nugent is an award-winning Innovation Leadership Coach with an outstanding track record, across generations, of mentoring aspiring students and employees into career and life success.

Kim brings forth over 30 years of consistent excellence in the field of management and leadership. With fine-tuned inspiration and stellar guidance, Kim collaborates with organizations to strengthen their workforce and delivers exceptional results. Kim provides professional-development services in the areas of leadership training, performance improvement, and talent enhancement.

Kim believes if you want to achieve extraordinary results, you must start with your people. Investing time, training, and mentoring to bring out the best in each individual is the first step in her proven "innovation leadership" process. The next step is to build a culture of sustainability built on values through a customized mentoring system to achieve changes in behavior and desired results. This does take time, but the results are worth it. Kim is passionate about helping people achieve personal, and career success through mentoring and coaching, which

KIM NUGENT, ED.D.

creates a journey towards designing lives without limits.

Dr. Kim Nugent is also a best-selling author of the following books: *Did I Say Never?, 52 Weeks to Exceptional Leadership, and Promotion Protocol: Unlock the Secrets to Promotability and Career Success.* Kim was recently awarded the prestigious **Top Innovation Leadership Coach of the Year 2019** award by the International Association of Top Professionals (IAOTP).

Kim has a Doctorate in Education from the University of Houston. She also has three Masters Degrees — an M.B.A. from St. Thomas University, an M.S. in Instructional Design and Online Learning from Capella University, and an M.S. in Human Resources Management from Keller Graduate School of Business. Her undergraduate experience earned her a B.S. degree in Hotel and Restaurant Management from the University of Houston, Hilton College. Kim lives in Houston, Texas.

• •

For keynotes and other speaking opportunities, training, customized workshops, break-out sessions, and leadership retreats, please contact Dr. Nugent at Kim@DrNugentSpeaks.com.

For Paving Your Path mentoring program inquiries, please contact at Kim@PromotionProtocol.com.

• •

ALL OF KIM NUGENT'S BEST-SELLING BOOKS ARE AVAILABLE WORLDWIDE VIA AMAZON & INGRAMSPARK.

www.ingramcontent.com/pod-product-compliance
Lightning Source LLC
Chambersburg PA
CBHW051350290426
44108CB00015B/1950